THE COMING GREAT REVIVAL

The Coming Great Revival

Recovering the Full Evangelical Tradition

William J. Abraham

1817

Harper & Row, Publishers, San Francisco

Cambridge, Hagerstown, New York, Philadelphia
London, Mexico City, São Paulo
Singapore, Sydney

FIRST EDITION

Library of Congress Cataloging in Publication Data

Abraham, William J. (William James), 1947-
   THE COMING GREAT REVIVAL.

   Includes bibliographical references and index.
   1. Evangelicalism—United States—History—20th century.   I. Title.
BR1642.U5A27 1984   280'.4   84-47710
ISBN 0-06-060035-7

84 85 86 87 88 10 9 8 7 6 5 4 3 2 1

To
Shaun R. F. Cleland

Contents

Acknowledgments

This little tract for the times began life in a vigorous discussion I had with Dr. Frank Spina, professor of Old Testament at Seattle Pacific University, in the summer of 1980. I had just arrived in Seattle to take up teaching duties at Seattle Pacific University and was gradually adjusting to life in America. Dr. Spina's thesis was attractively brief: evangelicals are really "fundamentalists with good manners." At that time I was convinced that evangelicalism should be distinguished from fundamentalism, but Dr. Spina's challenge forced me to explain the difference between the two. This was far from easy to do but I tried as best I could. As I have explored this further I have had to think very hard indeed both about my own intellectual history and about the history of evangelicalism. I have come close to agreeing with Dr. Spina about the most recent phase of the evangelical heritage. Yet I am convinced that there are versions of the heritage that can be distinguished from modern fundamentalism and its recent offspring, conservative evangelicalism. Moreover I believe that it is very important that such versions be cultivated over the generations. In what follows I seek to make my own modest contribution to that process.

I could never have written this book without the help and support of a host of people. At one time or another I discussed the issues involved with Frank Spina, Eugene Lemcio, Robert Wall, Larry Shelton, Dan Berg, Bruce McKeown, Donald Dayton, Walter Helsell, Uel Dunlop, Stafford Carson, Kent Hill, Frank Gourley, and David Livingstone. I thank them all for their kindness. A special word of thanks goes to James Barr, who read an early draft and encouraged me to go on with the work. I do not discuss his fascinating and entertaining account of recent evangelicalism in what follows, but I have learned much from it. A special word of thanks also goes to Roy M. Carlisle of Harper & Row, San Francisco, whose editorial assistance has been invaluable.

Several people helped with typing. I want to thank Sonya Vasilieff, John Spady, Barbara Rodgers, and Sharon Morrison. Sharon also made some incisive comments on the last three chapters.

Through it all my family have provided essential support and relief, so my thanks go to Timothy, Siobhan, Shaun, and above all Muriel, my wife. I could never have made it to the end without them.

1. Owning the Evangelical Inheritance

One hallmark of a civilized people is that they possess some sense of the historic traditions that have shaped their formation. This book is an attempt to understand the nature of the evangelical tradition, which over the years has had a profound and lasting impact on many Christians.

Acknowledging the Past

By tradition I mean that network of beliefs, attitudes, and ideals that is handed down through the generations. Evangelicals are extremely reluctant to acknowledge the positive significance of tradition in theology and piety. They naturally construe scripture and tradition as rivals. Being firmly committed to the former, they see tradition as a human construction with a built-in tendency to contaminate or eliminate the pure Word of God. This is in part a reaction against the claims of Roman Catholicism, which they believe has set tradition on a par with the Bible and has therefore bred gross theological error.

This negative evaluation of tradition is reinforced by prevailing cultural attitudes. It blends well with a general reaction against tradition as something old-fashioned and outdated. Traditional ways are set against modern ones; the latter, being new, are expected to be better. Moreover, within the field of education, it is often assumed that the ideal to be sought is individuality and autonomy. The expected outcome is an autonomous individual self-consciously making his or her own decisions unrestrained by past tradition. From within this ideal, attention to past tradition will seem to be suspiciously akin to escapism or will be taken to betray a lack of intellectual courage and fortitude. It will be viewed as the by-product of a weak mind that is bereft of any sustained, creative ideas. In turn, any attempt to explore tradition will seem like a rationalization of the status quo or a matter of pedantic interest.

Within Christianity, commitment to tradition is often seen as the great obstacle to progress in ecumenism. If Christians would only either give up or modify their traditions, they could come together in one new body for united action in the world. Fidelity to tradition fosters suspicion, fanaticism, and intolerance. Adherence to tradition is egocentric, self-serving, and contrary to God's call to unity and love. Or so it is thought.

It is easy to find evidence for the bad effects of tradition. We have all seen it, so it would be tedious to cite the details. Yet the negative results are only half the story and we need at the outset to dwell on the inescapability and value of tradition.

As conservatives in any walk of life are correct to point out, tradition has this in its favor: it has proved its worth over the years. It is not for nothing that the old ways have survived; new ways are often passing fads. Moreover, tradition and autonomy are not necessarily opposed to each other. Creativity and individuality require a context for their development and expression. In fact, one becomes autonomous not by bypassing tradition but by going through and then beyond it. You cannot, for example, become a competent musician or scientist by living on a desert island. Even learning to speak requires initiation into a community. Moreover, good fruit will not grow in bad soil, so examining the soil is not pedantic; it is sound common-sense.

As for ecumenism, it is short-sighted to set it against a positive evaluation of tradition. Ecumenism does involve change but it does not require that tradition be destroyed. Those who have no tradition of thought and action to share with other Christians are often barren. Like it or not, it is those who care about their heritage and who appreciate that of others who have most to contribute to any discussions about the unity of Christendom.

In any case, people do not become Christians in a vacuum. They are inevitably initiated into a living tradition that informs and nurtures their faith and practice. The must used analogy of "new birth," beloved by evangelicals, makes this plain. When a person is "born again" into the family of God, it signals the beginning of a new Christian life; the new babe in Christ has to learn to walk and talk. A whole new life of thought, feeling, and action is begun and then developed over time. Just how this life is developed depends crucially on the tradition of those people who nurture the new Christian in the faith. One has only to observe how converts take on the style of the Christian group they join to confirm this point. They simply imbibe, almost as if by osmosis, the lifestyle, piety, theology, and liturgy of those who succor them in the faith. Sometimes even language and mannerisms betray the source of the tradition into which they have been initiated.

Of course not all Christians go through a dramatic conversion experience, nor should they, for it is folly to identify what the New Testament writers call "new birth" with dramatic conversions. Many people find themselves in homes where from their tenderest years they loved Christ. They are no less "born again" than those who wandered in the far country before returning to the Father. To be "born again" is to enter into right relationship with God and this can take place by any number of different psychological paths. However, the point at issue still stands. Whatever one's personal experience, the structure and character of one's faith is shaped and provided by that tradition in which one finds oneself. Tradition, therefore, is absolutely fundamental to the ordering of our Christian existence. It is naive and insensitive to deny this.

We can make much the same point this way. Christians are inescapably rooted in and tied to communities of faith of one sort or another. To be sure, to be a Christian is to belong to the church universal. However, the church universal subsists in the various public communities that make up Christendom. Thus to join the body of Christ, one cannot avoid joining some concrete, particular body of believers at some particular place in time and space. To claim that one belongs to the church universal but that this does not entail belonging to some specific body of believers is a sham and an evasion of the demands of Christian obedience. It is at heart a rejection of the communal character of Christian existence; one cannot join the Christian community without being involved in some *particular* Christian community. These particular communities are not just physical entities of brick and mortar; they are expressions of Christian tradition. They are identified and constituted by the ideals and convictions that underlie their history and development. Thus to explore the Christian tradition that has shaped and continues to shape one's life of faith is a matter of profound though indirect importance.

Valuing the Legacy

A healthy religious tradition is therefore a precious heritage we neglect at our peril. There are several ways in which a religious tradition functions positively for our good. First, it provides a means of identity by relating a person's convictions and aspirations to a stream of ideas, people, institutions, and movements that stretches into the past and reaches out into the future. It thus provides a kind of reference for locating oneself on the map of conflicting ideas and ideologies that are such a persistent part of life. Second, a tradition provides a network of explanations that embody explicitly or implicitly the ultimate assumptions through which we perceive reality. A tradition invariably draws these assumptions and explanations into a rounded whole and expresses them through media as varied as hymns, sermons, creeds, formal ritual, moral insights, tracts, and theological treatises. Moreover, a tradition provides a moral and intellectual grid for evaluating our behavior and goals, for assessing new ideas, and for understanding and assimilating new discoveries. Third, a tradition provides psychological and social support to cope with the great crisis of life. At times of anxiety, a healthy tradition provides invaluable means for sustaining a fragile existence. Thus at birth, puberty, and death, during marriage, illness, and old age, a tradition can provide through its members, its rituals, and its intellectual resources a rich fund of experience, illumination, and hope to draw on. Those who ignore this fact are either impoverished in their understanding or sheltered in their experience.

Furthermore, a tradition acts as a womb for the creation of new ideas and fresh construction in theology. This makes a heightening of the importance of tradition a priority for theology at present. It has become commonplace to emphasize that pluralism, if not confusion, is the order of the day. In such a time, one useful way forward is to become deeply steeped in the theological traditions of the past. Fresh breakthroughs may come from exploring the full potential of a rich tradition that has existed over the centuries but whose current phase may be reaching the point of exhaustion. Certainly this is what seems to have been happening in the works of major revolutionary figures like Augustine, Aquinas, Calvin, Wesley, and Barth; tradition provided the soil for fresh development and theological construction. Unfashionable as this may be now, it could well constitute the one hope of reaching the other side of the present period of transition.

Finally, a sound and sensible tradition will save Christians from fanaticism. It will nurture them in the classical faith of Christendom and thus provide balance and depth to their vision of God and the world. It will give their children space to breathe and grow spiritually. It will provide resources for necessary rebellion and reform. It will transmit a wisdom that spans the ages. It will inspire patience to grapple with those tangled and demanding issues each generation must face in its own unique context. It will provide a bulwark against the incipient paganism that always threatens the people of God.

Above all, in a real but mysterious way, it will even give us access to Christ himself. After all, the One Christians serve is not just a figure from the past; he is the risen Lord present among his people to save and sustain. Just as the Son of God came to us incarnate in Jesus of Nazareth, so the risen Christ comes to us afresh incarnate in his body, the church, complete with its diverse traditions. Thus to think on those traditions in which he has visited and redeemed us is to gaze on holy ground. There is no place for fanaticism in that kind of company. There is plenty of room for greater clarity and circumspection than we presently exhibit.

Discovering the Evangelical Tradition

Many will agree with this positive evaluation of tradition, but they will wonder whether it applies to evangelicalism. Non-evangelicals do not generally view the evangelical tradition as either sound or sensible. They may admire its zeal, its interest in personal piety, its skill in evangelism, perhaps even its interest in scripture. Yet few contemporary theologians consider the evangelical tradition a genuine source of theological reflection or spiritual renewal. The prevailing image of this tradition is that it is anti-intellectual and emotional, reactionary and restrictive.

What cannot be denied is that there is an evangelical tradition there to be explored and then either appropriated or rejected. This need not be argued, for a spate of books, theses, and articles have appeared on evangelicalism of late. There is a wealth of material discussing at length its history and character. No one can deny the rediscovery of a complex, noisy, dynamic tradition.

Despite this, there is considerable confusion about what the evangelical tradition is, even among historians and theologians. The very term "evangelical" sounds offensive to many and attempts at definition easily engender anger, frustration, or boredom. Those scholars with sufficient patience to hope for further light on what evangelicalism is invariably look to deeper and more detailed historical research as a way out of the present impasse. There is enormous gain in this approach to the problem; further historical work is needed and I hope that the next decade will furnish its own harvest of creative endeavors. However, it is unwise to believe that this will really resolve the issues clustering around the quest to understand what the evangelical tradition embodies and expresses. Historical research is but one of several approaches that should be nurtured if there are to be more than modest gains.

In this book I plan to examine the evangelical tradition as a philosophical theologian. Purely formal descriptions of what this involves are bound to sound abstract, if not pompous and alarming. Suffice it to say at this point that I am especially interested in three distinct issues. First, I want to explain the inner theological dynamics of the tradition as a whole. Second, I want to evaluate the content and nature of the tradition, seeking to explore and expound some of its resources for today. Third, I want to identify and resolve some general problems in the present expressions of the tradition that prevent it from making a full and healthy contribution to the life of the church. To be sure, the range of discussion will inevitably spill beyond these boundaries, but these questions delimit the primary focus of the work. I hope that this kind of inquiry can find a natural place alongside other approaches (historical, sociological, etc.) currently being pursued.

Contesting the Content

Before outlining my central theses it is pivotal that we appreciate the contested character of the evangelical tradition. We must abandon the common belief that the evangelical tradition is one agreed upon, uncontested body of doctrine. That belief is clearly surfacing when evangelicals construe themselves as a thin red line of gospel-truth stretching back through Warfield, Wesley, Whitefield, Calvin, Luther, Augustine, and others, right back to the apostles and Christ himself. The picture is that of a brief and agreed core of doctrine held intact initially by the church universal and then preserved pure by a faithful remnant in the modern world. This belief, which I am rejecting, also surfaces in the common means used to identify the evangelical tradition. The standard procedure is to draw up a list of essentials or fundamentals that are the essence or heart of the tradition. Both insiders and outsiders adopt this ploy, and, although it has its place, its limits have not been sufficiently recognized.

First, the idea of a thin red line stretching back neatly through the ages is an illusion. There is continuity over the ages but it involves brokenness, renewal, and change. This is not grounded on some relativist theory of history; it is grounded on hard historical fact, as we shall see. Second, there is no agreed upon list of essentials. Any informed student knows this; even the most superficial reading of the available literature will prove it beyond a doubt. Yet even though many acknowledge both these points, they rarely face the full implications of them.

Evangelicals themselves are very reluctant to acknowledge them. They know from bitter experience that their tradition will not survive if they abandon its core doctrines. They quite rightly point to evangelical movements, like the Student Christian Movement (SCM) in Britain, that have died within a generation when they abandoned a healthy regard for sound doctrine. Theological liberalism does not generally reproduce itself and hence those evangelicals who have a sense of history put much store by a stable core of doctrine that will transmit the faith across the ages. It is entirely natural for them to focus on a core group of doctrines as the essence of the tradition.

Once this is set in motion, revision is seen as defection and standard protective procedures are adopted. Everything from name-calling to excommunication is tried to preserve purity. It is easy for revisionists to yield to this pressure, for they, too, generally accept the assumption of an unchanging core, and honesty bids them accept that they have abandoned the tradition and should go elsewhere for sustenance. Some outsiders observe this process with considerable glee and develop complex theories about religious movements to explain it. Others wax eloquent about the marvelously dynamic nature of religion and make calls for an end to static commitments.

This whole approach to evangelicalism and its attendant consequences is not so much wrong as superficial, naive, and insensitive. Perhaps its greatest error is that it construes religious labels as descriptive. It looks on evangelicalism as a religious commodity that can be suitably canned and placed alongside other religious traditions on the shelf of history. This is hopelessly wrong. Defining a religious heritage from within is only marginally a descriptive exercise; fundamentally it is an attempt to sum up the central riches of the tradition; hence it is inescapably normative in character. In offering a definition of the evangelical tradition, one is picking out those elements that represent what is crucial and integral to its present and future well-being.

This immediately explains the disagreement about the list of essentials. Different exponents of the heritage focus on different aspects of the tradition as a whole. It also explains the past diversity. Thus the term "evangelical" meant one thing during the Reformation; it meant another in the period of the eighteenth-century revivalists; it means something else today. Great figures like Luther, Calvin, and Wesley are not replicas. They represent profoundly different accounts of a complex vision of the Christian tradition. The heritage they express and articulate is inescapably contested. There is quite literally an intense debate and contest about how best to develop and explain its essential ingredients. Once this contest is rejected, or once it degenerates into factionalism, or once it ceases, then the tradition is dead.

What holds the various expressions together as one tradition is not one agreed set of doctrines; rather unity resides in family resemblance. Despite differences of emphasis and expression, there is sufficient common appearance for both outsiders and insiders to identify a single evangelical tradition within the Christian tradition as a whole. It is this, not detailed agreement in essentials, that justifies the descriptive use of the label. But beneath the description there is an intense informal contest about its very soul and substance. The tradition itself is essentially contested; from one generation to another various figures arise who either launch new models of the tradition or so skillfully develop old models that differences in definition become commonplace. To see this is to be liberated from naive readings of the past and to be summoned to greater efforts of analysis and expression for the future.

Three Major Theses

A contested reading of the evangelical tradition lies behind all that follows. I aim to advance three major theses. First, I shall show that just at the point when modern evangelicalism has become respectable it is falling apart theologically. Second, I shall argue that this is to be expected when one examines both the roots and internal structure of modern evangelical theology. Much recent evangelical theology is an inadequate attempt to rescue the doctrinal content of early twentieth-century fundamentalism; this is a fascinating experiment but it has failed as a serious theological proposal. Third, this failure should not unduly perplex evangelicals. They need to abandon neither their honorable past nor their esteemed identity. Within the life and thought of John Wesley there lies a viable model that can act as a stimulus for modern expressions of the evangelical tradition. Moreover, merely recognizing that Wesley constitutes one model of an essentially contested tradition has much to teach us in the immediate future.

2. The Rise of Contemporary Evangelical Orthodoxy

If the evangelical tradition is a contested tradition, then there can be no neutral description of its central doctrines and convictions. Moreover, any core set of doctrines picked out as the essence of the tradition will be a matter of considerable dispute. Yet we need not despair of understanding the tradition. There are clear-cut, identifiable models of the tradition that can be readily described objectively. One such model worthy of sustained examination is provided by contemporary evangelical orthodoxy. Modern evangelicalism is not, of course, a monochrome, colorless entity, for there is internal conflict about its true identity. Yet candid observers will find the ensuing description accurate if not comprehensive. The natural place to begin is to trace the relationship between modern evangelicalism and fundamentalism.

The connection between modern evangelical orthodoxy and fundamentalism is so intimate that many use the terms interchangeably to refer to the same phenomenon. The historical reasons behind this practice are complex but indispensable for understanding the modern evangelical scene. The key to the story is to be found in the fact that a group of young, aggressive, well-educated, and talented fundamentalists, spearheaded by Billy Graham, quite deliberately used the word "evangelical" to describe the new version of fundamentalism they sought to proclaim and defend in the fifties. Their innovation was so successful that the brand of evangelicalism that emerged has become the standard by which the content of evangelical theology is currently measured within self-confessed evangelical circles.

The Doctrines of Modern Fundamentalism

The fundamentalism out of which the current evangelical orthodoxy emerged is an intricate and controversial phenomenon. Those with a passing knowledge of modern church history quite readily and indeed rightly associate it with a militant movement in America in the twenties that went forth to war against those who had sought to accommodate the content of Christian theology to the new ideas that convulsed the church in the nineteenth century. Many people, however, find the term so distasteful that they use it simply to condemn any religious or even political tradition they dislike. Until recently, even scholars tended to dismiss fundamentalism as a reactionary, rural development unworthy of sympathetic attention. Now, fortunately, it is receiving the attention it deserves and, as a result, its religious and doctrinal character can no longer be ignored. For present purposes all we need is a brief summary of its theological agenda.[1]

A religious movement of any strength tends to be a coalition of diverse and even contradictory interests. This is certainly true of fundamentalism. Moreover, the very character of fundamentalism tends to breed discontent and conflict even within its own borders. It is held together as much by what it opposes as by what it proposes. In its classical period in the twenties, it took the form of a crusade resolutely opposing modernist and liberal theologies. The latter, in the eyes of fundamentalists, were to be found wherever theologians had accepted the results of biblical criticism or the theory of evolution. It did not matter, at this point, that theologians might want to accept these developments because they were true or even that those who did so argued that they were fully in keeping with their evangelical faith; in fact, the latter group were seen as guilty of especially odious betrayal of the faith. The mere willingness to consider biblical criticism or evolution as live options was greeted with hostility and opposition and constituted sufficient grounds for separation. True believers were to separate from

unbelievers, from apostates, and even from believers who asso-
ciated with what were believed to be modernists or liberals. In
the most formative period, fundamentalists expressed their
separatist convictions by seeking to purge the churches at large
of those who did not share their theology; later on when this
failed, separation took the form of complete withdrawal to form
rival churches and organizations. Even yet the debate about
what separation means is not over.[2] Some argue that separation
should be from unbelievers only; others adopt a more stringent
policy, insisting on separation from those who will not separate
from unbelievers; others argue that one can associate with believers in the mainline denominations so long as one is helping
them to separate therefrom; still others argue for separation in
religious work but contend for cooperation in politics.

The debate about separation within fundamentalism is an
expression of the ecclesiology of the movement. Fundamentalists are committed to a purist doctrine that emphasizes that the
church should consist only of those who are true believers. The
latter are identified by their having been "born again," one of
the marks of which is commitment to a strict body of finely
tuned "orthodox" beliefs. Thus their ecclesiology cannot be divorced from a wider network of theological convictions that
tend to be grouped under the heading of basic fundamentals of
the faith. These consist of the verbal inspiration of the Bible as
originally given, resulting in complete inerrancy in all that it
says, the virgin birth of Christ, his substitutionary atonement,
his bodily resurrection, and the authenticity of biblical miracles.
These five points of fundamentalism, as they came to be
known, constitute a firm core of the tradition, but they are but
part of the total theological agenda. Three other closely con-
nected elements deserve mention.

First, fundamentalists saw the present time as being very
close to the return of Christ. They therefore construed contemporary history as the prelude to the time when Christ would
return to earth prior to establishing a kingly reign of one thousand years characterized by peace, justice, and equity. This em-

phasis on the imminent return of Christ derived from a second element, namely, the tendency to interpret the Bible literally. The language of scripture was taken at face value and interpreted in plain, commonsense categories. This whole approach to the Bible in turn betrayed a naive realism at the philosophical level, for fundamentalists generally believed that our perceptual organs have a direct, unmediated access to the real world. Indeed this element in their outlook made it virtually impossible for them to appreciate the evidence for evolution, because they construed the theory of evolution as a kind of wild guess that fell far below the demands on an inductive science, which, for them, must be based on straightforward, plain observation of nature.

The fundamentalists' beliefs about the end time were also intimately related to a third ingredient in their theology, namely, their view of creation. Expressed most simply, they held that the human world is so corrupt that it can only get worse and worse. The present world is really under the sway of the devil; the most that God does is preserve a pure remnant; in due course he will move in to act in judgment to clear up the present unspeakable mess that pervades the institutions of Christendom and the world at large.

This complex doctrinal vision, when taken as a whole, generated a characteristic lifestyle and led to a spirit of controversy: the true believers must not only proclaim the truth, they must wage war against the enemy, if necessary dividing unbelieving institutions as much as possible. It also gave impetus to personal evangelism: as many as possible were to be rescued before they would fall into the hands of the devil. As D. L. Moody, one of the heroes of fundamentalists, sums it up: "I look upon this world as a wrecked vessel. God has given me a lifeboat and said to me, 'Moody, save all you can.' "[3] Not surprisingly, fundamentalists considered the social application of the gospel a snare and a distraction that would use up the energy that should be expended on evangelism. The work of evangelism itself made necessary the building and support of Bible colleges and encouraged churches and their leaders to develop revivalistic techniques to ensure that the gospel was preached and sinners were brought to decisions for Christ.[4] In more personal matters, fundamentalists stressed the importance of separation from such external sins as smoking, dancing, drinking, and gambling. Also, they expected to be persecuted and relished any opportunity to contend earnestly for the faith, not hesitating to be as outspoken and abrasive as circumstances required.

It is extremely important to see fundamentalism as a genuine doctrinal tradition. It embodies a particular reading of such central Christian themes as creation, the fall, salvation, church, consummation, and so forth. I am not claiming that it amounts to a serious theological tradition. The latter I would reserve for a genuinely critical, self-searching account of Christian doctrine. "Theological tradition" can only be applied to fundamentalism as a courtesy title. Fundamentalism is a populist doctrinal tradition expressed in hymns, tracts, and sermons. Many of its ideas take the form of propaganda cleverly developed on an ad hoc basis as the need arises. As a result, it is difficult for fundamentalists to stand together very long doctrinally. Yet its doctrinal character clearly needs to be acknowledged. In turn, contemporary evangelical orthodoxy should be seen as a theological reaction against fundamentalism. At its best, it should be viewed as a deliberate, well-planned attempt to reform fundamentalism and purge it of its more bizarre and obnoxious features. No account of it can overlook this fact; its very use of the term "evangelical" was adopted to further this goal.

Neo-Evangelical Revisionism

It might well be asked why modern evangelicals could not have rescued and redeemed the term "fundamentalist." The reasons for this are quite simple. To begin, the word "fundamentalist" had become such an odious term that only the most belligerent would dare use it. The ferocious fights within the mainline denominations, most especially within the Presbyteri-

an and Baptist traditions, the acrimonious debating and wran-
gling, and above all the total public fiasco displayed in the
Scopes trial of 1925 made the term a scandal and a joke.[5] Only
the most stouthearted or naive could continue to use the fundamentalist badge of identity. Walter Lippman's observations capture the issue very appropriately:

In actual practice, this movement has become entangled with all sorts
of bizarre and barbarous agitations, with the Ku Klux Klan, with
fanatical prohibition, with the "anti-evolution laws" and with much
persecution and intolerance. This in itself is significant. Such practice
shows that the central truth, which the fundamentalists have grasped,
no longer appeals to the best brains and the good sense of the modern
community, and that the movement is recruited largely from the isolated, the inexperienced, and the uneducated.[6]

In such circumstances it is only natural that sensitive souls
would cast around for an alternative designation.

A second reason for avoiding the term stems from the
changes that a younger generation of fundamentalists sought to
effect. They genuinely and self-consciously set about discarding
some key elements in the fundamentalist vision, which led, in
turn, to an authentic change in lifestyle. To explain this further,
we must explore the controversy that agitated fundamentalism
in the forties and fifties and turned it into an isolated movement until its resurgence in the late seventies. One of the key
figures in the change of direction was the well-known evangelist Billy Graham.

Graham began life as a fundamentalist. With his family he
attended the Associate Reformed Presbyterian Church, which
was separatist in its origins. Some time after his conversion he
was ordained into the ministry of the Southern Baptist Church.
For his education he attended Bob Jones University, then in
Cleveland, Tennessee, before moving on to Trinity Bible College, and then finishing at Wheaton College. All of these were
bastions of fundamentalist doctrine. For a while Graham
worked as a pastor in Illinois, but he quickly took up a traveling

ministry with Youth For Christ, conducting rallies in America and Europe. In 1947, Graham was appointed president of Northwestern Schools, a set of institutions founded by the stalwart fundamentalist W. B. Riley. Graham doubled as president and Youth For Christ evangelist for over three years until the workload became too heavy. Through all this Graham's fundamentalist credentials were impeccable. He worked in partnership with the leading fundamentalist figures of the day and publicly affirmed his fundamentalist convictions without hesitation or prevarication.

Later, in 1949, Graham was catapulted into the public eye during his crusade in Los Angeles, when the secular press developed considerable interest in his work. Following this and other mass rallies, many fundamentalists believed that a new day had dawned for their cause. This was not to be, however, for over the next seven years Graham embarked on a journey that took him out of the theological exclusivism of his past and into an inclusivist ecclesiology. Over time Graham deliberately rejected the separatist strand in the fundamentalist agenda. The most conspicuous expression of this was his welcoming support from nonfundamentalists in the crusade he held in New York in 1956. For fundamentalists this was the end of the line; for Graham it signaled a new beginning.

Graham, at this point, was part of a much deeper drift from fundamentalism, for others were also embarking on the pilgrimage that was to coalesce and form the evangelical orthodoxy of modern times. One of those was Donald Grey Barnhouse, a Presbyterian graduate of Princeton, who became in time a well-known journalist, commentator, and broadcaster and exercised an influential ministry from the pulpit of the Tenth Presbyterian Church in Philadelphia. In his early days Barnhouse had been a fundamentalist, going so far as to advise a young minister to shave his head if the hands of the elders and ministers of the Presbytery were to touch him in ordination.[7] Barnhouse was found guilty by the Presbyterian Church for charging another minister of heresy but, rather than leave, he

accepted the verdict and stayed within. In time he gave up his
separatist convicions and went on to champion the cause of the
World Council of Churches. He preached the gospel and spread
his ideas as editor of *Eternity* magazine. By the time of his death
in 1960, he was lauded most warmly by the liberal *Christian
Century.*

Chief among others who shared the road were such figures
as Bernard Ramm, Harold Lindsell, E. J. Carnell, Harold John
Ockenga, and Carl F. H. Henry. Together these provided the
theological and political expertise needed to rework the fundamentalist agenda for the postwar period. Part of the strategy to
achieve this was to change the label. Ockenga coined the term
"neo-evangelical" to describe the change of outlook. Sometimes the term "new evangelicalism" was used, but eventually
the word "evangelical" became sufficient to mark off this group
from its fundamentalist parent.[8] This shift was relatively easy to
effect, for even fundamentalists had often used the word "evangelical" for their own position. Besides, it was a label that had
been around for a long time in the history of the church and thus
had considerable prestigious connotations in the minds of conservative Christians. Moreover, fundamentalists, relishing the
smell of battle, quickly pounced on the new label as a quick way
of identifying the enemy and were happy to reserve the fundamentalist label for themselves. This, in itself, made it easier for
the new evangelicals to use the fundamentalist position as a
contrast to their own endeavors.

The success of the new evangelicals in forging and com-
municating their position is nothing less than amazing. Within
a short time they had a body of clear and closely argued literature, which earned the attention of academic theologians.
Ramm, Carnell, and Henry became, through their writings,
household names as spokesmen for the new brand of orthodoxy that became fashionable in evangelical circles.[9] Over
the years this group of writers and scholars expanded to include
a host of figures spanning two generations and stretching across
the ocean to Britain and throughout the world.[10] The movement

has produced a veritable wealth of material ranging from theological treatises to collections of articles, journals, dictionaries, introductory textbooks, and other lesser genres. Much of this material emanates from publishing houses that work exclusively for evangelicals and insist on certain doctrinal tests for their writers. Its theological vision has been projected across the world in the pages of *Christianity Today*, the magazine developed by Graham and others as a vehicle for the new movement. Moreover, the movement first had its own seminary in Fuller Theological Seminary in Pasadena, California, but before long a whole range of seminaries and colleges became neo-evangelical in their outlook.[11] In addition, neo-evangelicals found a ready outlet for their views in the National Association of Evangelicals (NAE), which was founded in 1941 and originally included leading fundamentalists like John R. Rice and Bob Jones, Sr., but which in time became predominately evangelical in its makeup, especially so when Rice and Jones withdrew to form their own organization. Fundamentalists, in so far as they could unite, gathered together in the American Council of Christian Churches. The picture that emerges, therefore, is that of a very deliberate, well-executed movement that broke with fundamentalism in the forties and fifties and became the evangelicalism the average person encounters today in the modern world, especially in America.

It must be remembered in all this that fundamentalism by no means disappeared. To be sure, it became isolated, but it lived on with its own leaders, literature, Bible schools, denominations, colleges, day schools, and magazines. As a religious phenomenon it has exhibited considerable staying power. Especially visible to the public eye were and are figures like Carl McIntire, Bob Jones, Sr., Bob Jones, Jr., Bob Jones III, John R. Rice, Ian R. K. Paisley, and Jerry Falwell. Fundamentalists have made extensive use of television and radio, have engaged in widespread missionary activity, and have kept alive the basic doctrines that have been its pride and glory from the twenties. Of late the most significant development has been the move to work quite openly in the political arena.[12] How far this will affect the internal content of fundamentalism over the long term is anyone's guess.

The Theology of the Neo-Evangelicals

An intriguing feature of the new evangelical movement of the fifties is its theology. George Dollar's definition of evangelicalism is a useful point of entry to this. He defines it as:

An attitude or position which professes to adhere to the Fundamentals of the Faith but advocates a spirit of re-examination of the basic doctrines, an attitude of tolerance toward the Liberals and an entering into "dialogue" with them, and an emphasis on the love and mercy of God rather than on His holiness and righteousness.[13]

What this observation accurately records is that the new evangelicals had the unenviable task of holding to some of the core convictions of fundamentalism while discarding its more unpalatable ingredients. This is a difficult experiment to execute, as we shall see. The basic mode of change was that of subtraction and addition. The new evangelicals kept the basic five points of the fundamentalist creed, discarded its separatist ecclesiology and some of its literalism, were more flexible about eschatological fine tuning, and added what they could of social concern. Out of this emerged a relatively coherent and stable theological vision that provided space for changes of tone and of lifestyle.

A most significant change was the rejection of the separatist ecclesiology. Graham was especially decisive and influential in this area, for it directly affected his work as an evangelist. At the convention of the National Association of Evangelicals in 1957 in Buffalo, New York, he left no doubt as to where he stood. Defending his practice of working with nonfundamentalists, he said:

First, as to its sponsorship, I would like to make myself quite clear. I intend to go anywhere, sponsored by anybody, to preach the Gospel of Christ, if there are no strings attached to my message. I am sponsored by civic clubs, universities, ministerial associations and councils of churches all over the world. *I intend to continue.* Not one person in New York has even suggested or hinted as to what my message should be. It will be precisely the same message that I have preached all over the world. The centrality of my message will be *Christ and Him crucified.*

Second, we have been challenged on what happens to the converts when the crusade is over. Apparently these brethren who make these statements have no faith in the Holy Spirit. The work of regeneration is the work of the Holy Spirit. The work of follow-up is the work of the Holy Spirit. The same Holy Spirit that convicted them of sin and regenerated them is able to follow them. No group of ministers in any large city anywhere in the world agrees on what constitutes a sound church. We do all we can in follow-up, but ultimately they're in the hands of the Holy Spirit.[14]

Behind this lay an inclusivist view of the church rather than an exclusivist one.

The one badge of Christian discipleship is not orthodoxy, but love. There is far more emphasis on love and unity among God's people in the New Testament than there is on orthodoxy, as important as it is.

We evangelicals sometimes set ourselves up as judges of another man's relationship to God. We often think that a person is not a Christian unless he pronounces our shibboleths and teaches exactly the way we do. I have found born again Christians in the strangest places, under the oddest circumstances, who do not know our particular evangelical language. But their spirit witnesses to my spirit that they are truly sons of God. There is a great swing all all over the world, within the church, toward a more conservative theological position. The old terms, fundamentalism and liberalism, are now passé. The situation has radically changed, since the days of Machen, Riley and other defenders of the faith a generation ago.[15]

Admittedly, Graham does not enunciate any positive doctrine of the church, but his ideas are far removed from those of conventional fundamentalists.

The same applies to the attempt to encourage evangelicals to pursue the social implications of the gospel, a move especially canvassed by Carl F. H. Henry, who became the leading theologian of modern evangelicalism.[16] Henry constantly chided fundamentalists for their obsession with petty externals and called on new evangelicals to address the modern world by developing an adequate social conscience and adorning their commitment to orthodoxy with deeds of love. Christians were to help others in a practical way and they were to remove suffering, evil, and injustice. Thus social responsibility was to become a Christian necessity, not an optional extra.

This reflected a much more optimistic view of the world, compared to that of fundamentalism. The world was not so dreadful and corrupt that it could not be partially redeemed by Christians at work in society. In turn, this called for a drastic change of emphasis in the field of eschatology. New evangelicals continued to insist on the Second Coming of Christ, but a broad range of options was tolerated.[17] Some even advocated the classical postmillennialist view that before Christ returns there will be a time of peace and justice for all. This change made it possible, in due course, for evangelicals to tolerate a more figurative interpretation of various parts of scripture. This was especially the case in the interpretation of the early chapters of Genesis. Ramm, for example, initiated a major controversy and discussion within evangelical circles when he argued that the theory of evolution could be a live option. Ramm, in fact, felt that so long as evolution was seen as a biological theory and not a metaphysical account of creation, it was "as harmless as, say, the relativity theory."[18]

Throughout all this, the new evangelicals held resolutely to other central convictions of fundamentalism. In fact, they took great pride in their theological orthodoxy and were at pains to distance themselves from liberalism and neo-orthodoxy. Sometimes they gave the impression that fundamentalists were entirely acceptable theologically. Fundamentalists were, in the words of Harold Ockenga, "noble men, committed to orthodox Christianity, who suffered at the hands of ecclesiastical modernism."[19] Unfortunately, however, they had allowed the ridicule and persecution heaped upon them by liberals to make them suspicious and schismatic.[20] This indicates very clearly that there was very substantial theological carry-over from fundamentalism into evangelicalism. Especially conspicuous in this is the doctrine of biblical inspiration. Evangelicals simply adopted the position developed by Warfield and his forebears and on this point followed the fundamentalist line in toto. Thus evangelicals have clung passionately to inerrancy and have either opposed historical criticism vehemently or sought to tame it and bring it under theological control. Alongside this they continue to insist on such points as the virgin birth and bodily resurrection of Christ, his substitutionary atonement, and the reality of biblical miracles.

Evangelical Theology in Britain

So far I have concentrated on developments in America, but it is helpful to note briefly what happened in Britain. The end result is much the same, but the journey has been less dramatic.[21]

Britain never had the kind of theological battle between fundamentalists and modernists that took place in the twenties in America. If one uses the rise of the Inter-Varsity Fellowship (IVF) as a pointer to the development of modern British evangelicalism, then the picture that emerges is one of steady growth and expansion. There was a break within evangelical ranks. There were those, represented by the Student Christian Movement, who refused to develop a clear body of doctrine and who as a result found themselves ultimately without any support. Over against these, those who formed groups like IVF gradually became a major force for evangelical Christianity both in the universities and in the churches. The favored internal designation for these is that of conservative evangelical, the label generally adopted by those who wanted to be less open to the modern world.

Initially, there was not too much opposition to the word "fundamentalism." J. I. Packer could define it with favorable overtones, suggesting it stood for the basics or fundamentals of the Christian faith.[22] Over the years, as people became more informed about the events of the twenties in America, it clearly became more difficult to use this term without inviting odious comparisons. Some outsiders would still like to pin the label on modern evangelicals, but once we become aware of the real character of fundamentalism, it becomes increasingly difficult to do this.

The chief reason for this derives from the real similarity and close links between British and American evangelicals. From the beginning, British evangelicals rejected a separatist ecclesiology. In student circles, evangelicals did of course insist on separation, but this was not an ecclesiastical principle. Groups like IVF were not seen as churches; hence evangelicals could with consistency argue for staying within the main denominations. Moreover, British evangelicals held to a strong doctrine of inerrancy, construing this as a critical element in a wider set of orthodox doctrines. Hence there was an agreed upon core of theology along with an internal weighting of the elements in that core. Also, British evangelicals had no real objections to social involvement, they did not insist on a detailed eschatological program, and from the outset they strove for academic responsibility in their publications. The similarities between this theological package and what emerged under the inspiration of Graham, Henry, and others are obvious. So it is small wonder that links were formed: British and American evangelicals stood for a common cause. For both, Graham was clearly the evangelist par excellence. Moreover, there was much mutual admiration. On the British side, writers like Henry, Ramm, and Pinnock became well known; on the American side, Stott, Packer, and Lloyd-Jones became household figures. The similarity between British and American evangelicalism is a remarkable development. Given the differences in culture and the differences in the historical roots of both traditions, it is surprising how close British and American evangelicals are to each other theologically. Of the two, the American version is the more volatile and flexible; because of this, I shall now examine it more closely.

Summary Conclusion

In the course of this chapter I have sought to establish that there is in the twentieth century a version of the evangelical tradition that can and should be distinguished from fundamentalism. The figure who, in the public eye, represents this tradition, both in Britain and America, is undoubtedly the evangelist Billy Graham. Around and behind him are ranged a whole network of theologians, student organizations, publications, educational institutions, publishers, and even churches. Theologically, the evangelicalism expressed by Graham and others is close to fundamentalism, but it is sufficiently different from the latter to merit attention and evaluation on its own terms. Any responsible account of the evangelical tradition must reckon with the changes Graham helped to initiate. To see them as mere window dressing is to ignore the sophistication and courage exercised by a body of able and astute religious figures in the recent past. It is easy to dismiss these leaders and innovators as just "fundamentalists with good manners." Some were of course just that and we shall have occasion to note in due course that the modern evangelical movement failed to extract itself sufficiently from fundamentalism. But if we are to sustain this assessment, it should only be *after* we have acknowledged the radical division that took place within fundamentalism in the fifties. Those who broke from that tradition have a right to use the term "evangelical"; perhaps they, more than any other group, are responsible for the continued use and popularity of the label.

The break between evangelicalism and fundamentalism was certainly more marked in America than in Britain. Initially British evangelicals could construe themselves as fundamentalists without undue embarrassment. However, as they began to co-operate with American evangelicals and as they became better acquainted with the actual history of fundamentalism in the twenties, they too wanted to disassociate themselves from that tradition. This was entirely natural, for they, like their American friends, genuinely rejected crucial elements in fundamentalism.

Two consequences follow from this reading of the tradition. First, we should avoid casting suspicion on the motives of modern evangelicals in their break from fundamentalism. The new evangelicals, as a whole, genuinely sought to interact in a responsible way with other theologians, and they authentically desired to shed some of the worst features of their fundamentalist past. To achieve this was no mean feat and it deserves to be fully recognized. Second, we should be careful not to explain away the rise of modern evangelicalism in purely sociological categories. It is true, of course, that part of the explanation of the change of direction should be traced to the changed social and political circumstances of the postwar period. The new evangelicals may well have been moving up in the world and thus needed to shed the old fundamentalist image. However, hard evidence for this is by no means available and such evidence as exists is susceptible to contrary interpretations. In the meantime we should not be shy of construing the modern evangelical vision I have described here as genuinely theological in nature. Theology may not be modern evangelicals' best gift to the church, but they have had a distinct theology of their own, which deserves to be criticized rather than disdainfully ignored.

3. The Collapse of the Modern Evangelical Experiment

Contemporary evangelical orthodoxy is a bold attempt to redeem the doctrines of modern fundamentalism from unwelcome associations. How successful is this experiment? In this chapter I argue that it faces an internal crisis unlikely to be resolved by further tinkering from within. As a result, evangelicals need to turn to radically alternative models of their own heritage if they are to find a way out of the present crisis.

Initial Signs of Trouble

That there is a serious crisis within evangelicalism is indicated by several factors. To begin, evangelicals are no longer certain who they are or what they should believe in certain crucial areas. The label, which had been such a rallying point in the fifties, has become so qualified that it has ceased to be attractive. Joseph Bayly, writing in *Eternity* magazine, a bastion of recent evangelical orthodoxy, has even confessed that he is resigning from the evangelicals.[1] He finds evangelicals adding accretions to the tradition that leave him ashamed and embarrassed. The accretions in mind include: Jerry Falwell's citing palatial success as a mark of divine favor; Wheaton College excluding Jews, Buddhists, and Muslims from its student body; and Bailey Smith, the Southern Baptist leader, claiming that God does not hear the prayers of Jews. Bayly also mentions the recent emergence of various evangelical action groups, like the Moral Majority, which stand for a right-wing political platform. To avoid such associations Bayly proposes dropping the term "evangelical" altogether and calling himself a Christian.

Bayly draws attention here to one aspect of the crisis among evangelicals. Despite all their efforts, modern evangelicals still have difficulty in separating evangelicalism from fundamentalism in the public eye. There are good grounds for arguing that these two movements can be distinguished, as I indicated in the last chapter, but the differences are not widely known outside American evangelical circles; hence the two tend to be lumped together indiscriminately. As a result, when authentic and self-confessed fundamentalists like Jerry Falwell become well known, it is very difficult for the average person to see the difference between him and an evangelical. In fact, Falwell becomes for many the model of the true evangelical, a development somewhat embarrassing for modern evangelicals.

The crisis modern evangelicals face is, however, not of the kind that can be resolved by skillful public relations. It runs much deeper. What is ultimately at stake is whether the modern evangelical experiment initiated by figures like Graham and Henry has succeeded or failed as a coherent, theological vision of the Christian faith. One possibility to be faced is that contemporary evangelical orthodoxy is still too much indebted to its fundamentalist past to be tenable. Thus the present search for a viable form of evanglical identity is a clear sign that the noble experiment of the last generation is in serious theological trouble.

Misgivings along these lines were expressed by neo-evangelicals themselves at a very early stage. Influential members of the National Association of Evangelicals were not at all sure about the new developments charted by Graham and his defenders. Many of the rank and file were uneasy about concessions made to science, ignored the new social ethic advocated by Henry, and remained deeply suspicious of neo-evangelicals. A succession of leaders were also uneasy about what was happening. In 1958 Paul Petticord, the founder of Western Evangelical Seminary, was worried that evangelicals would give up the fight against liberalism, fearing that efforts to coax them back into the mainline churches by the neo-orthodox would contaminate their orthodox faith.[2] In the same year, G. Aiken Taylor, who became vice-president of NAE in 1973, expressed concern that solid evangelical unity would be lost by realignment with those who used the language of orthodoxy but supposedly did not really believe it.

No greater time of danger has come upon the Christian Church than the present. For today Faith cannot be distinguished from Doubt by the language it uses or the confession it makes. Unbelief once kept itself aloof from the household of faith. Today it wants to come into the house, take a place at the table and crawl into bed with the children . . . without becoming a member of the family.

This is the situation which has driven Christians of every faith to a re-alignment of their loyalties. A new evangelical ecumenism is rising to meet the rapid ecumenism of radical theology. . . .

Thus instead of fading into disuse, such tests as the so-called five points of fundamentalism may loom in increasing importance.[3]

A year later, Stephen Paine, a president of NAE, wondered if the new movement was sufficiently different from its predecessor to merit a new label. His argument was quite simple: "Is new-evangelicalism different from evangelicalism? If so, is it still evangelical? If not, why bother with a meaningless appellation?"[4]

One reason why some fundamentalists went through with the transition was straightforwardly pragmatic. The new movement provided scope for greater influence, even if it did put at risk one's theological integrity. Besides, Graham is a very charismatic figure whom it is difficult to dislike as a person, and once he made the transition, others naturally followed, allowing their hearts to melt any arguments that might have been advanced by their heads. Some were candid enought to say that accepting modernist support for the Graham rallies was one way to help meet expenses. W. K. Harrison, an army general and a contributing editor to *Christianity Today*, argued along such lines and openly confessed that cooperation with modernists did not involve fellowship with them.

The desire of and consequent invitation by the Protestant modernists to receive Mr. Graham's ministry is certainly to be desired in the interest of saving men's souls. . . . The use of unbelievers' money to pay the necessary expenses of the meetings which they themselves seek seems logical and legitimate to me. That modernists may be on the committee or sit on the platform are not in themselves evil, as I see it. I believe any real believer would welcome an invitation to preach the true Gospel to the pastor and unsaved people in a modernist church. . . . Yet, if one accepts such an invitation, he does so from the pastor of the church, and that pastor will sit on the platform and probably take part in the service.

There is in this no recognition of any yoke or Christian fellowship. . . . Now, I see little difference other than in magnitude between the preaching of the Gospel in a single modernist church and in New York by Billy Graham.[5]

Thus, from the outset, modern evangelical orthodoxy had within its ranks genuine, old-fashioned fundamentalists who only reluctantly, if at all, went along with the revised version of the tradition advocated by Graham and others. Such a movement is inherently unstable and is therefore unlikely to remain intact under severe pressure. Over the years the pressure has increased steadily.

Political Upheaval

One significant source of tension stems from the political and social upheavals that occurred in America in the sixties. The wave of social protest expressed in the civil rights movement, the revulsion against the Vietnam war, the discovery of oppressed minorities, and the disillusionment with authority that came to a climax in the rejection of Nixon after Watergate were convulsive in their impact. The bastions of evangelical orthodoxy either stood aloof from these issues, as they worried and fussed over petty personal matters like dancing and card playing, or they threw their weight behind the reactionary conservatism that defended the status quo. When they did eventually change, it was more because of outside cultural pressure than because of the internal content of their theology. In such circumstances the call to develop a social conscience so loudly proclaimed by evangelical leaders sounded hollow and hypocritical. Younger evangelicals, when they thought about it, saw a complete failure of nerve and interpreted this as a serious disregard of the biblical mandate to pursue justice. Those who did not leave evangelicalism found themselves ill at ease in Zion.[6]

Sometimes the criticism of younger evangelicals was derived from a startling rediscovery of alternative wellsprings of the evangelical tradition that lay beyond the fundamentalism of the twentieth century. Neo-evangelicals were rather dogmatic and sometimes grossly insensitive about the history of the evangelical tradition. Among their heroes were, of course, figures like Warfield and Machen, scholars who provided crucial theological ingredients in the fundamentalist creed. In rejecting fundamentalism, neo-evangelicals felt they were simply repudiating accretions that had besmirched what good fundamentalists stood for. However, neo-evangelicals sincerely believed they were also carrying on the great traditions of Luther, Calvin, Wesley, and the like. Younger scholars, sensitized by the events of the sixties, found it impossible to accept this claim and for very good historical reasons. Thus Donald Dayton has shown that strands in the evangelicalism of America in the nineteenth century were deeply committed in practice to justice and equality in a way unheard of in fundamentalism and modern evangelicalism. People like Charles Finney and groups like the Wesleyan Methodists were committed to the poor and to women to a degree that would shock and embarrass their later descendants.[7] These later descendants vigorously censored the offensive elements in Finney's writings: when they edited and reprinted his works, they excised those passages that call for radical social reform. Dayton is here uncovering a significant version of the evangelical tradition in the last century that had been ignored or distorted by his own heritage and that was, to some degree, in keeping with the Wesleyan tradition of the eighteenth century. This discovery functioned as a kind of time bomb that exploded the framework of the evangelical faith in which he had been reared.

While Dayton has looked to his roots within and around the American Wesleyan tradition, others found similar inspiration in the Calvinist tradition. A notable example of this is the developments currently being pursued at the Institute of Christian Studies (ICS) in Toronto. The point of conflict that sparked change in this case was the discovery that modern American Calvinists had gone along with their evangelical brethren in accepting a clear separation between church and state. A group of younger scholars, believing that this was a sell-out to secularism and drawing on the theology of Dutch Calvinists, vehemently repudiated this. Insisting that Christians should be involved in politics in a direct fashion, they founded their own political party in Canada (after testing this possibility in the courts) and opened the ICS to propagate and develop their ideas. The pain and upheaval that this involved was considerable.[8]

These discoveries and the events that prompted them have had a threefold effect. First, they caused considerable disillusion among younger evangelicals. Evangelicals had sought to become socially responsible, but they failed in practice when put to the test. Second, they laid bare alternative accounts of the evangelical tradition and thus enabled many to revolt against the recent past without repudiating wholesale the tradition in which they had come to faith. Third, they forced evangelicals to look again at their theology. Interestingly, the key issue demanding attention was one that evangelicals have long neglected, namely, ecclesiology. The move on the part of neo-evangelicals to abandon a purist doctrine of the church has ironically come under severe fire. Great efforts were made in some circles in this period to develop a model of Christian community that would embody the radical demands of Christian discipleship.

The Problem of Inerrancy

Another area of tension within modern evangelicalism stems from the unease about inerrancy. If any single doctrine has been considered sacrosanct, it is this one; yet it has been the cause of untold discussion and debate. The time, money, and energy spent on holding the line in this area must be staggering. Yet the battle rages on.

The debate itself has not centered on exegesis or even on issues in systematic theology. The issue has been historical: what has the church believed about the scriptures? This is a very blunt instrument for resolving a very complex theological problem. Yet the battle continues with hardly a pause for breath between rounds. The most conspicuous and lengthy treatment of the issues clustering around inerrancy is *The Authority and Interpretation of the Bible* by Jack Rogers and Donald McKim.[9] This was a response to the charges made by Harold Lindsell, who had accused the faculty of Fuller Theological Seminary of having abandoned a truly evangelical doctrine of inspiration.[10] Rogers and McKim have argued that there is a central church tradition on scripture that is different from that developed at Princeton in the last century by Warfield and his predecessors. Materially, they claim that the church has always held that the Bible is entirely trustworthy for matters of salvation rather than technically or scientifically correct in all that it affirms. Their opponents reject this and are currently at work on a series of projects intended to show that the church has always held that the Bible is inerrant in all that it says.[11]

Both sides in this debate have gotten the history wrong. First, there is no central church tradition on inspiration. No single theory will do justice to the diversity of opinion among past theologians on revelation, inspiration, authority, and inerrancy. Even within the thought of the great individual theologians there are serious tensions and contradictions they did not resolve. This is all the more evident when one consults a wider range of figures. Second, many central theologians were very definitely committed to a theory of divine dictation, which modern evangelicals have themselves violently rejected. The standard ways to avoid acknowledging this are very simple. One reads the past to ferret out every conceivable reference to inerrancy but quietly ignores any reference to dictation. Or, if one does acknowledge the references to dictation, one skillfully explains them away by pretending that they are mere metaphors. Blinkers and prejudice govern the interpretation of the past in such cases.

What is ironic in all this is the implicit appeal to church tradition. Of course, there is more behind inerrancy than the appeal to tradition, but this is not what strikes one when reading modern evangelicals. The whole debate is cast much more in pre–Vatican II Roman Catholic categories than it is in self-confessed evangelical ones. Everything is made to revolve around elaborate historical discussions about the past tradition of the church. When that tradition is itself misconstrued, then the whole approach is damaged beyond repair.

Nowhere is the bankruptcy of modern evangelical theology more conspicuous than in this domain. The one issue on which it has staked its life has been handled in an insensitive, narrow, prejudiced, and alien fashion. What must be honestly confessed is that the doctrine of inerrancy is intimately related to a doctrine of divine dictation that is now gone forever. The modern doctrine of plenary inspiration is in the end nothing more than an ingenious way of holding to inerrancy when its roots have been repudiated. All the historical scholasticism one can muster, all the technical theological dexterity one can develop, all the highbrow hermeneutical skill one can deploy—none of these can undo this fact.

Evangelicals, of course, are not keen to drop inerrancy. Inerrancy is constitutive of the modern experiment, so it is difficult to give it up. However, it is eqally difficult to combine inerrancy with two other crucial elements in modern evangelical orthodoxy. Thus it requires enormous wisdom to be committed to inerrancy and at the same time to be committed to modern science and history. The whole enterprise is doomed to failure because the latter entail canons of judgment that are radically distorted or undermined when combined with inerrancy. Moreover, it is inevitable that there will be conflict between what evangelical scholars believe and the results of responsible scholarship. As a result, evangelicals will be seen as expending endless energy on defending the Mosaic authorship of the Pentateuch, the single authorship of Isaiah, and an early date for Daniel, when what is needed is to move beyond even the critical consensus on such issues and explore more fully what scripture means and how it is to function as canon in the life of faith. Thus, like it or not, evangelicals committed to inerrancy find it very difficult to receive a ready welcome in the world of scholarship. Further, to do so, they have to qualify the term out of existence. Even that evokes distaste, for it invariably looks as if the only reason the concept is retained is that it allows one to say the password needed for admittance into the evangelical subculture, complete with its cluster of institutions, publishing houses, and journals. Generally these are white, middle-class organizations.[12] Inerrancy, therefore, is a barrier to the kind of dialogue and scholarly conversation neo-evangelicals sought to initiate when they broke with fundamentalism. It is hard to stitch responsible scholarship to the core of the fundamentalist creed without the threads disintegrating.

Inerrancy is also difficult to reconcile with another element in the neo-evangelical agenda, namely, tolerance toward others. One of the reasons why evangelicals cling to inerrancy is its role in the foundations of their theology. The general feeling is that if inerrancy is abandoned there is no control over what one may then believe. Somehow, one's theology will become subjective in the worst sense of the word. Given this, it is difficult to be entirely happy with those who reject inerrancy. Try as one may, one is constantly tempted to construe the rejection of inerrancy as the first step in the ultimate erosion or destruction of the Christian faith. In such an atmosphere tolerance is a virtue well nigh impossible to cultivate and practice.

Our review of the discussion about inerrancy leads us, therefore, to conclude that much modern evangelical theology has turned out to be barren. It has failed to pursue an adequate methodology in this area, focusing narrowly on historical issues. It has not gained respectability within modern scholarship. On the contrary, those who have ventured courageously into this arena have had to qualify the concept out of existence. Not surprisingly, they have then come under attack from within the evangelical fold. Tolerance has quickly given way to excommunication. Moreover, the whole debate about inerrancy has become sterile and scholastic. This in itself signals the bankruptcy of the tradition as a serious theological proposal. Inerrancy has proved to be a millstone around the neck of modern evangelicalism, drowning its riches in a sea of historical prejudice and an ocean of defensive theological rhetoric.

The Flowering of Scholasticism

This judgment is confirmed when one looks critically at the benchmark of systematic theology within evangelical circles, Carl F. H. Henry's six-volume work, *God, Revelation and Authority*.[13] This work represents the distillation of a whole generation's labor and has rightly been lauded as the most important work of evangelical theology in modern times. Henry, as we have seen, was one of the key architects of modern evangelical orthodoxy and he is generally regarded as the dean of evangelical theologians. Yet the climax of his work is deeply disappointing. One looks in vain here for a fresh, invigorating expression of the Christian gospel. There is nothing here that humbles the soul before God, drives one to Christ in fresh love and adoration, inspires one to love one's neighbor as oneself, or encourages one to preach more faithfully. Henry provides no deeply illuminating account of the human predicament and no penetrating analysis of how the gospel is good news to a broken world. There is no compelling account of Christ; there is next to nothing on the doctrine of Christian life or the work of the Holy Spirit in renewal; there is very little on the nature and demands of Christian community.

What we have instead is over three thousand pages of turgid scholasticism. Readers swirl around in a sea of names who are either called in defense as witnesses to the truth or carefully worked over as inconsistent heretics. A dead and barren orthodoxy decked out in a magnificent display of learning is presented as the riches of Christian faith. Even educated readers will soon find themselves suffering from either boredom or indigestion.

The work as a whole lacks balance. Four of the volumes are devoted to epistemological issues and develop fifteen theses about divine revelation. Henry stakes everything, therefore, on getting the foundations correct, but this proves to be so demanding and fragile that in the actual exposition of his theology there is really only time for the doctrine of God. Clearly no theologian can neglect these matters, yet to make them exclusively constitutive of theology is strange in the extreme. Moreover, the details are not very inspiring. In his doctrine of God, Henry repeats the traditional material without making it come alive for readers. In his epistemology, Henry articulates at length the fundamentalist position on special revelation, complete with its dogged adherence to inerrancy. In all, this represents a narrow, rationalistic analysis of the gospel. It buries the life of God, especially its personal dimensions, deep in an impenetrable, scholastic ideology. Those who look for a penetrating revival of the Christian heritage will find little to inspire and nurture them in these quarters. It is small wonder that many have felt uncomfortable in modern evangelicalism.

Regression to Fundamentalism

Some have found it so uncomfortable that they have returned to a classical fundamentalist position, abandoning the elements much praised by the neo-evangelicals. This is easier to do now because the charismatic leadership exercised by Billy Graham in the fifties and sixties is no longer as effective as it was then. Hence those who perhaps followed him for emotional and pragmatic reasons rather than because of theological conviction have no longer enough to sustain them in their commitment. Besides, fundamentalism, with its simplistic outlook and hard stand, is bound to become attractive when it becomes difficult to control what is happening among younger evangelicals. Old fears dormant for a generation flame forth into life in a moment. It is difficult to avoid this conclusion, although one must be cautious in choosing examples. A likely candidate is Harold Lindsell. Lindsell had been one of the architects of neo-evangelicalism at Fuller Theological Seminary and for years served as editor of *Christianity Today*. In 1956, at the height of the dispute between fundamentalists and neo-evangelicals, Lindsell wrote:

Fundamentalism has been chastened so that it is sloughing off its reactionary character. It has become more positive. It now attacks the viewpoint, not the individual. A man may entertain whatever viewpoint he wishes and the fundamentalist may disagree with him without assuming that he is dishonest, a scoundral and one who should be hung from the nearest gibbet.[14]

Presently, Lindsell's work and activities bear most of the hallmarks he here repudiates. Within the last few years he has systematically exposed, attacked, and castigated those who have not been able to share his inerrancy shibboleth.[15] As a result, respectable neo-evangelicals use his position as a useful contrast to their own ideas in the effort to propagate a more responsible image. Perhaps it is no accident that Lindsell used the term "fundamentalist" as a designation for his own position; now at last he reveals his true colors; others gladly follow his lead.

Another likely candidate for regression to fundamentalism is Francis Schaeffer. Schaeffer has been something of a guru in modern evangelicalism and has had an influence far beyond what his ideas deserve. He is quite explicit about the need to return to the separatist tradition of the fundamentalists. "God is giving his people a second opportunity. . . . To take this opportunity means going back to the 1930s and picking up the pieces from the mistakes that were made then."[16] One piece to be picked up is the concept of the purity of the visible church. If the church is to be kept pure through the next generation, inerrancy must be maintained even if it is at the cost of severing fellowship with others.

We who stand for the Word of God as without mistake not only when it speaks of salvation matters but also when it speaks of the cosmos, history, and moral norms, must be careful to live under the Word we say we hold dear, and that very much includes love to those (many of whom are certainly brothers and sisters in Christ) who we think are at this time making a dreadful mistake in their view of the Bible. But love and personal fellowship does not mean allowing this view of the Bible to shape the next generation. If it does, the next generation will be swept away, and the church of Christ will have lost the absolute by which to judge or help the relativistic surrounding culture.[17]

Two other major figures who deserve mention are Wilbur Smith and D. Martyn Lloyd-Jones. In their case it is difficult to know whether they reverted to fundamentalism or whether they were just friendly fundamentalists who became more vocal and visible late in life. The latter is the more likely story. Both died only recently, admired each other enormously, and, through their Bible teaching, had probably more influence than any other pair in the last generation. Interestingly, neither had any formal theological training, a fact that makes their influence all the more remarkable.

Smith was a key figure in the development of Fuller Theological Seminary. He was one of the first faculty members to be recruited and worked diligently in helping to put it on the map. After sixteen years, however, Smith became very concerned about the direction of the seminary, being especially worried about ideas that had developed on the topic of inspiration. Rather than tolerate diversity on this issue, he resigned and went to Trinity Evangelical Divinity School.[18] The letter of invitation from Kenneth Kantzer, then dean at Trinity and until recently editor of *Christianity Today,* reveals very clearly that Smith was very much an adherent of more of the fundamentalist mind-set than is characteristic of neo-evangelicals.

First I wish to state more clearly than I did in my earlier letter how much we really need you and how much we feel your presence with us would mean for the Lord's work. You are, you know, a symbol of that for which we wish the school to stand—evangelical scholarship consecrated wholly to Jesus Christ *in a premillennial framework.* You are a vigorous man, and we believe that you could give us many years of spiritual and intellectual guidance. I don't wish to say more than I ought, but were you to throw your lot here at Trinity, I think you could give us as younger men the wisdom and direction that may enable us to avoid the mistake we most dread to make—to help us so that in creating a strong and powerful center of evangelical thought, we may not in the process lose sight of our real source of greatness, *the complete authority of an inerrantly inspired Bible.* We feel that in this, *as well as in our premillennialism and in our puritanism,* we are wholly one with you; and you would find yourself at one with us.[19]

Martyn Lloyd-Jones's position is even more illuminating. In the last generation he was the prince of expository preachers among evangelicals; no one rivaled him in stature, and from his pulpit in London he propagated a message that was carried overseas in his writings. In retirement he gave an interview with Carl F. H. Henry that not only expressed his profound disappointment at what had happened in the last generation but resurrected some classical fundamentalist doctrines.[20] He repudiated the ecumenical evangelism practiced by Billy Graham; he rejected the effort to reform the world pronounced by Henry; and he argued for an imminent eschatology complete with its radical pessimism about current events. He even confessed that he expected the world to end within twenty years. If this does not constitute a reversal to an unsullied fundamentalist position, nothing does.

Lloyd-Jones is not the only one to repudiate quite self-consciously theological elements in the neo-evangelical agenda. It is rather clear that the strong emphasis on social action propounded by younger evangelicals like Ronald J. Sider and Evangelicals for Social Action (ESA) is evoking a classical fundamentalist response.[21] John A. Sproule of Grace Theological Seminary has spoken unequivocally to this point. He believes that, practically speaking, it is quite impossible to reform the world; the kind of social concern Christians should display is markedly individual and personal in nature. What is especially revealing is Sproule's theological response to social action.

Theologically, the ESA seems hampered by an obvious naivete about God Himself and the direction in which He is moving all the events of history. It would seem Sider and his friends have given little thought to the fact that most of the starving millions live in dark paganism (Muslims, Buddhists, etc.) where the God of the Bible is rejected as the only true God and His Son, the Lord Jesus, is rejected as the only Saviour of men. All such persons, regardless of where they live, are under God's wrath continually (John 3:36). What they need, as a matter of first importance, is the light of the Gospel, not only to dispel spiritual darkness but, also, to enable them to become involved in self-improvement to correct social inequities within their own cultures. One might ask, what about the pagans who live in luxury in the more advanced nations? The answer is that they need the Gospel just like everyone else, but they are where they are because of God's providence. He is still sovereign and He does as He pleases with His world. He determines where people will be born and where they will live (cf. Acts 17:26, NIV).[22]

The social and political condition of the world will be radically improved only when Christ Himself returns to reign. Then, and only then, will true justice reign universally. It has never been God's plan in history to reconstruct a fallen world with fallen men. No *human* plan will relieve this problem. This does not absolve true believers from their individual and corporate responsibilities to live more simple lives and to give much more sacrificially of their material blessing to help others—but none of these endeavors, nor the models of ESA, will change the course of history as revealed in Scripture. World-wide hunger will be with us always.[23]

These developments surely confirm that contemporary evangelical orthodoxy is not as stable as it was thought to be. If the turmoil were caused only by pressure from without, this might be considered uneventful; after all, every tradition goes through periods of stress caused by external circumstances. However, it is a different matter when the turmoil springs right from within the tradition itself. As we have seen, much of the current debate and struggle stems from younger evangelicals who have discovered alternative roots of the evangelical heritage, who have found that they can be liberated by Christ without adopting much of the moral and theological baggage carried by neo-evangelicals, who have found considerable intellectual pain in following through on the consequences of inerrancy, and who have, as a result, been attacked by their evangelical brethren. On reflection, it is surely not surprising that the tradition is in turmoil, for it was never really stable from the outset. The present problems are simply the consequences of patching together diverse elements into a theological position that was never very coherent in its inception. The tradition was as much held together by dislike of bigoted fundamentalist tactics in relating to other Christians and common admiration for Billy Graham than it was by any profound theological vision.

To say this is not to say that neo-evangelicals have been stupid or unfriendly or un-Christlike. On the contrary, those who developed modern evangelical orthodoxy required enormous sophistication and sanctity to achieve what they did. My claim is that there are internal tensions and contradictions even the best hearts and minds cannot evade indefinitely.

The issue can be expressed in terms of a dilemma. Consider the charges leveled against modern evangelicalism by Lindsell, Schaeffer, Smith, Lloyd-Jones, and Sproule. If evangelicals construe these as a regression to a fundamentalist position, then it is obvious that significant figures in the tradition have reached the painful conclusion that the experiment initiated in the fifties has failed. On the other hand, if they construe these charges as the expression of a true evangelical stance, then they undermine the claim that modern evangelicalism differs in any substantial sense from fundamentalism. These options seem to leave modern evangelicals between a rock and a hard place. Either they must try to overhaul the ship of contemporary evangelical orthodoxy and launch out again on the journey charted by Graham, Henry, and others or they can man the old fundamentalist boats to face the encroaching storms before the end.

A Revisionist Alternative

It is worth pausing with the first of these alternatives for a moment. Of all the solutions offered, revising the present option must rank as one of the most important. What is really needed, some will say, is to take the modern evangelical ship back into dry dock, fit it out with some new equipment, and put to sea again. This is essentially the solution proposed by Robert Webber.

Webber is an interesting figure because he knows modern evangelicalism intimately from within and because he has written extensively on the need for renewal.[24] A graduate of Bob Jones University, he quickly found a home in modern evangelical orthodoxy and then became one of the moving forces behind the drive to break through to a more responsible expression of the tradition. He was a leading figure in the Chicago Call of 1977, which exhorted evangelicals to recover the fullness of the Christian faith.

This call to fullness is central to his solution to the present ills. Evangelicals need, says Webber, to embrace the full spiritual resources and the full doctrinal heritage of the Christian past. To achieve this, they must develop a new appreciation for the true nature of the church and a fresh awareness of the value of sacramental forms of worship. Theologically, evangelicals must become more aware of the classical theology of the past, especially of the early creeds as the key to interpretation of scripture. Moreover, they must develop a broader understanding of the mission of the church, including within that social and educational work as well as evangelism. Also, they must cultivate a deeper, more Christ-centered spirituality. In all, then, evangelicals need to recover the historic substance of the Christian gospel in thought, deed, and life.

Such a recovering does not involve any radical break with modern evangelical theology. The favored image is that of growth. Evangelicals need to grow beyond the present limits of the tradition toward a more inclusive version of Christianity. This does not involve taking issue with the doctrines of the current leaders. Webber is explicit on this: "We can affirm that we, as twentieth-century evangelicals, stand in continuity not only with the evangelicalism of the seventies, the sixties, the fifties, and the forties, but also with the fundamentalism of the thirties and twenties."[25] Webber therefore has no quarrel with inerrancy. Moreover, he shares the familiar opposition evangelicals display toward the Enlightenment and so-called secular humanism; little if any good can come out of these movements. Generally, he is entirely happy to endorse the prevailing evangelical orthodoxy as taught at Wheaton College, as proclaimed by Billy Graham, and as defended by magazines like *Christianity Today*.

Webber can do this because of his underlying account of the tradition. Basically, "evangelical" is a biblical term, derived from the Greek word ευαγγελιον. Fundamentally, an evangelical is anyone committed to the ευαγγελιον, to the good news of the gospel. The content of this is then worked out in detail so that over time it becomes possible to identify a specific body of doctrines that are constitutive of evangelicalism. Webber himself endorses a list of twelve doctrines satisfying this condition. The problem with many fundamentalists and neo-evangelicals is that they narrow their range of interest. True evangelicals will articulate a broad, comprehensive set of doctrines that will do justice to the Christian faith in its totality. Hence renewal involves recovery not repudiation.

Enough of Webber's position has been exposed to permit a critical evaluation of his proposals. On the surface these are very attractive and laudable. Problems, however, arise when one begins to examine them in detail. First, appeal to a biblical definition of "evangelical," although sanctioned by widespread usage, is misleading. Evangelicals, of course, will be reluctant to criticize Webber at this point, for they naturally like to appeal to scripture at every possible opportunity. The fact is, however, that etymology alone does not explain what is meant by the term "evangelical." There is no such thing as the biblical concept of "evangelical," at least not in the sense in which that term has come to be used by modern scholars. To be sure, evangelicals want to be true to the gospel as it is enshrined in scripture; indeed their passion to achieve this easily spills over into intolerance. They readily see themselves as the only defenders of the gospel; they are the true Christians; all others are counterfeit or half-baked Christians. But this settles nothing. Merely defining oneself as the true evangelical in some "biblical" sense provides only verbal warrants for a position that must be argued in detail. One must actually show that one's theology does justice to the gospel of Christ. This can, of course, be attempted, but claims about the meaning of the term "evangelical" or ευαγγελιον are of little help. Besides, just because "evangelical" may etymologically be related to the word "gospel," this does nothing to show that the use of the word "evangelical" is always related to the word "gospel." This is a clear case of the genetic fallacy and ignores the fresh meaning and new life a term may develop in different periods and cultures.

A second objection to Webber's analysis is that it tends to ignore the harsh reality of intensive conflict within evangelicalism itself. The picture he presents is a very congenial one. Differences in theological conviction are for the most part differences in emphasis. One group focuses on one part of the wider tradition, another group on another part. Differences arise between the various groups but they are not very significant; certainly there is nothing that a deeper awareness of the tradition as a whole should not elemirate. In this way conflict is minimized or eliminated entirely. This explanation of conflict is certainly an improvement on those views that perceive it as tied to weaknesses in the personalities or characters of evangelical theologians, but it is still inadequate. It does not do justice to the depth and intensity of internal conflict within the evangelical tradition.

Evangelicals cannot gloss over the deep differences that divide them. In the past they have been at odds over such central theological issues as predestination, divine inspiration, grace, eternal security, sanctification, the nature of biblical authority, the place of reason and experience in theology, the relation between evangelicals and non-evangelicals, and the relation of the gospel to science and historical criticism. At times evangelicals, of course, have agreed to live and let live on some of these issues. Moreover, they have generally agreed not to differ on such matters as the nature of church government or the place and significance of infant baptism. But this is only part of the picture. Evangelicals have at times differed vociferously and intensely over central theological convictions. Indeed, as we saw earlier, there is at present a major battle in progress over inspiration, a battle that brings to the surface considerable conflict over a large range of important issues. Webber's analysis comes nowhere near explaining this state of affairs.

Ironically, Webber himself has experienced the winds of controversy over his own proposals for the reform of the tradition. Thus David F. Wells has expressed grave misgivings over the Anglo-Catholic leanings reflected in his suggestions. Speaking to a group that undoubtably includes Webber, he remarks pointedly and bitterly:

I cannot be persuaded that we would be substantially better off venerating Catholic saints than pretty starlets, or that sober-faced genuflectors and swingers of incense are much to be preferred to the vacant worshippers some of our churches are creating. This may be a time of small happenings, of Pygmy spirituality, but a mass pilgrimage into the world of Anglo-Catholicism is not, with all due respect, what we need right now. Indeed, it is not what we need at any time.[26]

A third and crucial criticism follows. If the tradition historically is marked by conflict, then it cannot be corrected simply by adding in an extra element from the past where it suits. Hard decisions will have to be made about central theological issues. Within this some elements from the past will have to be repudiated. The neo-evangelicals themselves saw this in their break from fundamentalism, although they were reluctant to think this through. Not only that, the whole internal balance of the theology of evangelicalism must be entirely reworked. The obsession with epistemology has to be completely abandoned, while the weight given to the place of doctrine needs to be reevaluated. The native antipathy to the Enlightenment must be rethought, while greater efforts should be spent on cultivating serious biblical research, despite the risks involved. Webber is correct that a greater grasp of historical Christianity is needed. In particular, evangelicals badly need to develop adequate forms of piety, although precisely what these should be is an open question. But as they stand, Webber's proposals are cosmetic and superficial. What is offered is a timid rerun of the solution of the neo-evangelicals in the fifties. That tradition is now exhausted; not even a good dose of classical Christian doctrine will save it.

Conclusion

Modern evangelical orthodoxy is an inherently unstable theological tradition. The vision developed by the leaders of the last generation shows clear signs of internal collapse. Neo-evangelicals have not been able to disentangle their position very clearly in the public eye from fundamentalism, for some never really wanted to do that in the first place. The political upheavals of the recent past have disclosed profound internal conflicts in ethics and in ecclesiology. The debate about inerrancy has revealed that agreement on a doctrine of scripture has not materialized. It has also exposed very serious problems in theological methodology and made clear that biblical research is only marginally compatible with the canons of the tradition. Equally, it has made abundantly obvious that tolerance has very severe limits. Meanwhile the tradition as a whole has become more and more scholastic. Henry's *magnum opus* is the monument of a generation's work. When most evangelical publications have long been forgotten, all six volumes of it will remain as a landmark of the period. Yet given its barren orthodoxy and turgid character, it can at best inspire mediocrity.

In such circumstances, regression to fundamentalism is but a further sign that we have reached the end of an era. It reveals that even the present leaders have abandoned hope of redeeming the modern experiment. Patching in elements of the classical past to the fabric of fundamentalism has already failed, so there is little point in pursuing that option further.

Hope lies elsewhere. It lies in exploring a radically different model of the evangelical tradition. It lies in becoming deeply sensitized to the difficulties in creating new forms of tradition. It lies in acknowledging that theological and spiritual renewal is primarily a work of divine grace. To such matters as these we now turn.

4. The Radical Reorganization of Priorities

There is no easy solution to the present crisis facing the modern evangelical experiment. Minor adjustment in style or at the periphery of its theology are inadequate measures for the problems we have identified. It is highly unlikely, for example, that evangelicals are suddenly going to resolve their deep differences over social and political issues. Nor does it appear that evangelicals will find a way to reform and renew the church by the mere stroke of a pen. The issue of biblical authority will not be set to rights by more historical monographs ransacking the past for evidence for and against inerrancy. Deep questions about the interpretation and application of scripture will not be answered by further guidelines in hermeneutics. Debates about the foundations of knowledge will raise as many questions as they answer. Besides, who knows how to stop a tradition from degenerating into dull, orthodox scholasticism? Who knows how to inhibit regression into a narrow, arrogant, schismatic fundamentalism? Who knows how to prevent the development of a reactionary, vacuous, compromising liberalism?

Avoiding Hasty Panaceas

One of the major dangers facing modern evangelicals is that they will seek to heal their wounds too superficially. We know relatively well how to heal diseased and wounded bodies but not barren and diseased traditions. This is true for any serious religious tradition and stems in part from what a tradition actually is. Traditions are complex entities of thought and practice that are not under our direct control.[1] They arise we know not how; it is only by hindsight that we can chart their progress. They are handed down very often in imperceptible ways; they are as much caught as they are taught. They become stereotyped without our realizing it; they degenerate and die and those involved do not intend this. There is therefore no certain way to bring about their reform or renewal. We can offer our diagnosis and prescription, but there is no guarantee that the medicine will work.

Besides, the medicine may have unintended and unwanted side-effects. What reformers finally accomplish may be utterly different from what they set out to achieve because of the unforeseen effects of unintended circumstances or of factors outside their control. Traditions by their nature are not at our disposal to create or redeem at will. They are less like houses we can build and renovate according to plan and more like gardens we can seek to cultivate. We can prepare the ground, sow the seed, water the growing shoots, and prune the old plants, but the secret of growth, beauty, health, and fruitfulness lies elsewhere. That secret is not a human possession.

This is especially so with the evangelical tradition. Anything worthy of that noble name must express in word, thought, and deed the life of God in the human soul. Evangelicals at their best surely want to embody the gospel of Jesus Christ. To construe this as purely or primarily a human work is close to blasphemy. It cannot be done without the invisible inspiration of the Spirit of God. That Spirit is not for sale at any price. Not even evangelicals control where He comes from or whither He goes. This radically qualifies every effort of renewal and reform.

Displacing Intellectual Preoccupations

The irony at this point is that many modern evangelicals will agree with this. Many of them will be the first to insist on the role of the Holy Spirit in the renewal of the tradition. This naturally arises from their conviction that their own tradition is the product of divine grace. They sincerely believe that God has raised up evangelicals to rescue the gospel from apostasy, formalism, liberalism, and the like. Hence they will warm to what I am saying but be puzzled as to why I should see this as especially relevant.

My claim, however, is not that evangelicals do not believe in the work of the Holy Spirit but that their view of the Spirit's work is inadequate. On the one side, at the popular level, evangelicals so misconstrue the role of the Spirit that they have little or no awareness of the role of human factors in the origins of their own tradition. That is one reason why evangelicals are reluctant to speak of their own position or their own groups as actually being a tradition at all. Traditions are human in character; they are the work of human agency. But evangelicalism is a work of God; therefore, it cannot be a human tradition. Those who believe this will be very puzzled by my argument. They will simply see their activity as divinely caused and guided and ignore my appeal to look upon evangelicalism as a human tradition. They will be glad to know that the writer believes in the work of the Holy Spirit and then return to business as usual. They will miss the role that human factors have in the cultivation of the evangelical tradition and leave it to God and their leaders to see things through to the next generation.

On the other side, although evangelical leaders may *in theory* accept what I am saying, *in practice,* things work very differently. The tradition is looked upon most of the time as a vast industry that operates as a very human enterprise, requiring very human expertise to keep it going. Much of it is run as a very sophisticated business, complete with sales techniques, image makers, advertising experts, stage managers, directors, and the like. In all this, the Holy Spirit is relegated to the periphery, often invoked but seldom heeded.

More importantly, to accept my claim is to abandon the primary categories of the modern evangelical experiment. The leaders of that experiment have seen the primary problem of the modern church as theological in a formal sense. Everything has been predicated on right doctrine. Let the church recover and maintain the fundamentals of the faith, let there be a reformation of doctrine, then things will be set on the right course. This is what fundamentalists believe and modern evangelicals have not altered that emphasis. Indeed they adopted the fundamentalist obsession with inerrancy as the key doctrinal element without which all would eventually be lost. What modern evangelicals sought to do was to purge fundamentalism as a movement of its more bizarre associations and then graft on to its core of doctrines a social conscience, learned scholarship, good manners, a less schismatic view of the church, and other theological adjustments. The basic thrust of the fundamentalist tradition was not changed at all. Right doctrine was still the salvation of the church. In particular, the church needed to cling to and preserve the view of the origins of the Bible that had been so carefully articulated and defended by Princeton theologians of the nineteenth century. Modern evangelicals love, therefore, the image of intellectual foundations. The tradition is construed as a house of intellect, which must be built on sound epistemological premises. Hence the obsession with inerrancy.

Ironically, evangelicals share at this level much more of their opponents' assumptions than they realize. Liberals are not very different from fundamentalists and modern evangelicals in their commitment to the intellect as the cure for the ills of the church. They call for a rejection of fundamentalist doctrine and an acceptance of their own reformulation as the main hope for the future. Theology, conceived in a rather formal, academic sense, is seen as the way forward. The same could be said of many neo-orthodox theologians. T. F. Torrance and his followers, for example, have argued at length that a new theological science is the answer to the ills of modern evangelical theology.[2] What is remarkable here is the consensus on the primary categories. All agree that the fundamental issue is intellectual and epistemological.

Embracing Spiritual Renewal

What I am suggesting is that this concern with the intellectual and with formal theology be thoroughly relativized. It needs to be subordinated to spiritual renewal. We need to reorder our priorities so that the primary emphasis is placed not on right doctrine but on right relationships with God and with each other. The internal dynamic of the evangelical tradition must therefore be radically changed so that much more room is found for the role of the Spirit and the life of faith. Hence piety and obedience replace commitment to right doctrine as the essence of the evangelical tradition.

It is crucial that this proposal be understood correctly. I am not claiming that modern evangelical orthodoxy has rejected the work of the Holy Spirit as essential to renewal. My claim is that it has relativized the Holy Spirit by making its work dependent upon adherence to a rigidly defined orthodoxy. The latter is seen as the priority. Indeed the Spirit's role is construed as bringing home and applying the fundamentalist doctrines. Without these doctrines, the Spirit cannot work because it has little to do in the system but illuminate them within the human mind. And once the Spirit has implanted the doctrines, everything else will fall readily in place. This accounts for the intellectualist conception of the tradition as a whole and explains why even talk of renewal and revival rather than reformation is looked upon with considerable suspicion.

Moreover, in calling for a reordering of priorities I am not thereby castigating doctrine, formal theology, or even epistemology as irrelevant, unnecessary, or unimportant. My proposal can be expressed this way. I am suggesting that evangelicals put the renewal and re-creation of themselves and of all creation at the center of their outlook. When this happens, striving for correct doctrine is then a subordinate task that has a vital but not exclusive role in the working out of the heritage. More happily, I am proposing that we develop a much richer and more penetrating account of what true theology is. It is not a deductive science that simply organizes the propositions of the Bible. It is a fallible, human attempt to understand the intellectual content of the Christian faith. How exactly we develop this will depend on the audience intended and the end in view.

Part of the task at this level will be epistemological. We will seek to develop a coherent account of our knowledge of God, outlining within this what divine revelation is and how it relates to what we know about the world and ourselves from other sources. But these matters are highly debatable and controversial. There will be various ways of resolving the problems we face in this domain. Many of these will be entirely compatible with the gospel, so it is folly to make any one of them essential to the gospel itself. By relativizing epistemology and making it subordinate to the gospel, we are free to work in this realm as rigorously as we desire. Equally, we are free to embrace all those who share our quest for a deeper appropriation of the riches of Christ. This appropriation in turn cannot take place without deep repentance, without a radical openness to God, and without a penetrating work of the Spirit of God in the human heart. Within this, correct doctrine will find its place as one important factor in spiritual re-creation and renewal.

Finding a Suitable Model

By far the best way to explore this proposal is to look sympathetically at a version of the Christian tradition embodying this pattern of analysis. Amazingly, we do not have to leave the evangelical tradition itself to find what is in view. We can find such a version in the life and thought of John Wesley. In Wesley we have a splended model of the evangelical tradition at its best. Moreover, Wesley provides a radically different way of construing the internal content of the tradition from that provided by the recent past. By focusing on that model we can be liberated from the narrow confines of the last generation and introduced to a fresh and invigorating appropriation of the gospel.

To be sure, it would be easy to fall once more into the snare of looking merely to history for salvation. We could turn Wesley into one more hero who will lead us to the promised land. My aim is much more modest than that. I want to show that the solution proposed briefly in this chapter is not a pious hope. There has been in history a model of the tradition that has provided a much more penetrating expression of the evangelical heritage than the twentieth-century substitute. That in itself can be explosive in its effects. Moreover, by analyzing the relation between the Wesleyan and rival expressions of the heritage, we can think more coherently about how best to stimulate better expressions of the heritage in the future. We can also begin to make wise decisions as to what should be scrapped or retained in the present experiment.

Conclusion

Resorting to the gardening analogy, I can express my intention this way. I want to expose a section of the evangelical landscape that has been overshadowed by the cedars of recent history. That section has its own internal structure, its own plants and trees, it even has its own weeds and compost heap. Examining these matters will no more renew the evangelical heritage than will writing manuals about gardening grow roses. But it will broaden our horizons concerning what is possible and may even inspire us to take appropriate action. If in the process we continue to hold that we can somehow redeem the evangelical experiment without divine grace, then we have only ourselves to blame. We can break up the ground, tear up the weeds, plant seeds of truth, fence out the wild animals, and share our dreams of the ultimate landscape. We cannot of ourselves either fully predict the outcome or control the secrets of life and growth. These things are in the hands of God the Father, God the Son, and God the Holy Spirit.

5. The Wesleyan Version of the Evangelical Tradition

The classical Wesleyan expression of the Christian tradition offers a refreshing alternative to the standard models of the evangelical heritage currently available. In this chapter I sketch the central characteristics of Wesley's thought and, where relevant, draw attention to other facets of his life and work. Even then I cannot hope to be comprehensive. Fortunately, this should not worry us unduly. For one thing, excellent summaries of Wesley already exist and there is no point in duplicating the worthy efforts of others.[1] For another thing, nothing can replace acquaintance with the outstanding primary sources we possess. Wesley left us a wealth of material, so much in fact that he could distinguish within it between the canonical and noncanonical.[2] This chapter is then an account of the general structure and flavor of Wesley's outlook in which there are at least seven different strands to his genius.

Wesley's Approach to Theology

First, there is Wesley's whole conception of the theological enterprise. He is, as Outler points out, a folk theologian.[3] He articulates the fullness of the Christian message in plain words for plain people. He writes as a servant of the people of God, directing his energies to those matters that impinge on their pilgrimage of evangelism and service in the culture and context that they inhabit. His works therefore are inevitably occasional pieces directed to specific issues of the day. The most natural vehicle of this approach to theology is the sermon, although Wesley is sufficiently versatile to use to good effect such other forms as tracts for the times, extended essays, notes on the biblical tradition, dialogue, and open letters.

In all this Wesley is more akin to Luther than he is to Calvin, although Calvin's *Institutes* are in reality a brilliant attempt to provide the newly formed Protestant movement with a theological vision that would enable it to organize and appropriate its fresh discovery of the gospel. More significantly, Wesley is much closer to the kind of theology we have in the Bible. There is the same absence of systematic or formal apparatus. Thus the final redactors of the Pentateuch bring together a body of diverse religious traditions gathered from their own and their neighbors' heritages to expound in story form their vision of the world, of themselves, and of God and his revelation to them. The end product is truly astounding. It can retain the attention of the scholar, who is driven by its discrepencies, anomalies, and literary mysteries to attempt to unravel its origins in the ancient world. But its lasting value is attested by its ability to nourish the spiritual pilgrimage of the community that devoutly and prayerfully reads and ponders its content.

Scripture does not lend itself easily to formal systematic presentation. Somehow it has pleased God to leave this to those servants of his with a special gift in this regard. Wesley was not one of those. He focused on the more interesting and useful task of addressing those issues having an impact on the life of faith in his day. This is not to say that Wesley was indifferent to the complex philosophical and theological questions to which every theologian must sooner or later attend, if only in an informal manner. On the contrary, a very attractive feature of his work is the broad foundations that undergird his thinking.

The Wesleyan Quadrilateral

Much recent evangelical thinking has adopted the view that all our theology is built on one foundation and one foundation only. Everything in the end must be related by direct observation to the text of scripture or deducible from observations of scripture. This is thoroughly naive, not the least because it ignores the crucial role that tradition has in our theology. Wesley's multiple appeal to scripture, reason, experience, and tradition—what is called the Wesleyan quadrilateral—is a welcome alternative to this model of the theological task. There is, of course, a primacy to scripture in Wesley's thought, as we shall see. What is refreshing is the subtle placing of this in a wider context that does not exclude a responsible openness to past theological reflection in, say, the Fathers, and to new discoveries in, say, science and history.

Our debt to the Fathers is enormous. The central evangelical affirmations of the Trinity and the incarnation have for the most part been adopted unconsciously from them. Wesley's love and respect for the Fathers matches this admirably. Moreover, as I have acknowledged elsewhere, Wesley's openness to philosophy and reason has had a significant influence on my own attempt to develop an account of divine inspiration that will relate naturally to both the canons and results of the historical study of the Bible.[4] As to science, there is a passage in Wesley that is intriguing when one considers the futile debate over evolution that continues to rage in evangelical circles.[5]

There are no sudden changes in nature: all is gradual and elegantly varied. There is no being which has not either above or beneath it some that resemble it in certain characters, and differ from it in others. . . . From a plant to man . . . the transition from one species to another is almost insensible. The polypus links the vegetable to the animal. The flying squirrel unites the bird to the quadruped. The ape bears affinity to the quadruped and the man. . . . By what degrees does nature raise herself up to man? How will she rectify this head that is always inclined to the earth? How change these paws into flexible arms? What method will she make use of to transform these crooked feet into supple and skillful hands? The ape is this rough draft of man: an imperfect representation which nevertheless bears a resemblance to him, and is the last creature that serves to display the admirable progression of the works of God! There is a prodigious number of continued links between the most perfect man and the ape.[6]

Wesley was, to be sure, often quaint in his beliefs. He believed, for example, that before the fall, nature was devoid of blemish. Moreover, given his empiricism, it is unlikely that Wesley would have appreciated the complexity of modern scientific concepts, theory, and evidence. What is inspiring, however, is the critical, creative, and imaginative spirit that breathes through his writings. Everything, be it philosophical, scientific, or historical, is grist for the mill of his theological deliberations. Faith is not sealed off in a ghetto of revelation, indifferent to such truths as are available by common grace to either all humankind or to the humble scholar.

Yet faith is very fundamentally built on one's own experience of God. Nothing can take the place of one's own pilgrimage in which God reveals himself inwardly by the Holy Spirit. This is not just a vague awareness of God; it is not some abstract sense of the numinous in creation; it is personal experience of God's love in the cross of Christ for oneself as a penitent sinner. Thus it is best described as evangelical experience of God in a strict sense, wherein the Holy Spirit mediates, through the preached word of the cross, the love of God for the sinner as a single individual. Without this, religion remains formal and rather abstract; it remains a hope rather than a present reality.

The Primacy of Scripture

At the same time Wesley does not yield an inch on the central significance of the Bible for faith. Thus in his advice on study to a young lady, while enjoining a list of subjects including grammar, arithmetic, geography, logic, ethics, science, history, metaphysics, poetry, and divinity, he suggests that these should be a complement to the study of the Bible. After three to five years of such a diet, the results would be admirable.

... You will then have knowledge enough for any reasonable Christian. But remember before all, in all, and above all, your great point is to know the only true God and Jesus Christ whom he hath sent.[7]

The concluding remark is a key for unlocking Wesley's insistence on the primacy of the Bible. For him it is a crucial means of grace. It provides indispensable information about God and what he has done for humankind's salvation, so it is a critical factor in coming to know and love God. Everything else we learn needs to be incorporated into this relationship.

You want to know God, in order to enjoy him in time and in eternity. All that you want to know of him is contained in one book, the Bible. Therefore your one point is to understand this. And all you learn is to be referred to this, as either directly or remotely conducive to it.[8]

Those contemporary historians of Wesley who insist that he does not fit the fundamentalist paradigm are wise to explore this in detail. What is central to Wesley is the indispensable special revelation enshrined in the Bible. In this he is at one with classical Christian thinking and I have argued at length elsewhere that this is a vital ingredient for any sound expression of the Christian heritage.[9]

Yet Wesley never allowed this emphasis on the centrality of revelation to govern the material content of his theology. He was convinced scripture was essential; indeed he held that it was dictated by God. Yet in his sermons, the central themes engaging him are the new birth, justification by faith, the witness of the Spirit, sanctification, and so on. Wesley's primary concern is that we be immersed not in theories about the origins of the Bible but in the Bible itself. Nowhere does he make the doctrine of inspiration an essential part of the total content of the gospel or as a condition of fellowship. His desire is that we be open to the Holy Spirit as he takes the good news of Christ and brings it home to our hearts. Without this experience of the Spirit, the scriptures are a dead letter of no avail.

We can go further. Wesley develped an extremely sophisticated epistemology. He married in one creative synthesis the empiricism of Locke to the idealism of the Christian Platonists. The synthesis he in turn integrated with his favored interest in faith and the witness of the Spirit. It would be exaggerated to make Wesley into a philosopher, but it would be equally un-wise to dispute his considerable philosophical dexterity. He knew how to outline and define the details of his rich noetic structure. Yet again, nowhere does he impose this on others. He argues his case in detail and then leaves readers to think it through personally. Above all he realizes that it is the gospel itself and not the underlying theory of knowledge he personal-ly feels best explains and supports it that matters. The epis-temolgy has been firmly kept in its place as subordinate to past divine revelation and to the present work of the Holy Spirit. This is no mean feat.

A Moral Vision of God

A fourth element to be isolated is the profound and compre-hensive moral vision of God that pervades so much of Wesley's thinking. The heart of his faith is the all-embracing love and goodness of God as embodied in the unsearchable riches of Christ. This acts as a control on his thinking in such areas as predestination, Christian assurance, and providence.

His objection to unconditional predestination as he found it in Calvin and his followers rested not simply on its simplistic analysis of all the biblical material related to it. He also objected to it because it called into radical question the love of God for all humankind.

So ill do election and reprobation agree with the truth and sincerity of God! But do they not agree least of all with the scriptural account of his love and goodness: that attribute which God peculiarly claims wherein he glories above all the rest? It is not written, "God is justice," or "God is truth" (although he is just and true in all his ways). But it is written, "God is love" (1 Jn. 4:8) (love in the abstract, without bounds), and "there is no end of his goodness" (cf. Ps. 52:1). His love extends even to those who neither love nor fear him. He is good, even to the evil and the unthankful; yea, without any exception or limita-tion, to all the children of men. For "the Lord is loving" (or good) "unto every man, and his mercy is over all his works" (Ps. 145:9).[10]

It is the same theme that undergirds his insisting that people can really know whether they are in right relationship with God. The prejudices against this idea were as strong in Wesley's day as they are today. People naturally associate assurance with pride, presumption, and arrogance. Wesley was well aware of this. At stake for him was the love of God, a theme central to his sermon on the spirit of bondage and adoption. The very idea of adoption makes it clear that what is at issue is whether God loves us enough to adopt us as sons and daughters, so that we become not just servants of God but children of God. For Wesley, one who has received the Spirit

. . . cannot fear any longer the wrath of God; for he knows it is now turned away from him, and looks upon Him no more as an angry Judge but as a loving Father.[11]

Wesley's emphasis on providence also bears eloquent witness to the centrality of the love of God in his theology. This is best illustrated in some verses where he pours out his heart in protest against God, following the tragic episode where his brother, almost treacherously, deprived him of his bride-to-be, Grace Murray. Charles deliberately stepped in and had her married off to one of Wesley's friends and colleagues, John Bennett. Wesley's moving response begins in despair and ends in trustful resignation.

> O Lord, I bow my sinful head!
> Righteous are all Thy Ways with Man.
> Yet suffer me with Thee to plead,
> With lowly Reverence to complain:
> With deep, unutter'd Grief to groan,
> O what is this that Thou has done?
>
> Teach me from every pleasing Snare
> To keep the Issues of my Heart:
> Be Thou my Love, my Joy, my Fear!
> Thou my eternal Portion art.
> Be Thou my never-failing Friend,
> And love, O love me, to the End![12]

A Holistic Vision of Christian Witness

Given this emphasis on God's love, it is not surprising that there is no dichotomy between evangelism and social work. This is not even an issue. The love of God demands and inspires love of neighbor and that calls for action on every level that will meet his or her many and varied needs. Wesley led the way in this himself. His evangelistic labors went hand in hand with political, social, and educational activity. Most notable in this respect was his opposition to slavery, "that execrable villany which is the scandal of religion, of England, and of human nature."[13] It is well known that on his deathbed Wesley wrote to Mr. Wilberforce, urging him on in his attempts to bring slavery to an end.

Wesley was a pragmatist in his approach to social issues. He had no grand theory of society, no ideological blueprint to correct everything at a stroke. He worked piecemeal as the occasion arose but recognized that disciplined, planned, communitywide effort was needed if the people's problems were to be resolved. Thus he organized various schemes for the sick, for widows, and for orphans.

It is also worth noting that Wesley's ideas and practice had a profound indirect effect on social issues. His emphasis on the universality of sin and salvation was a great social leveler. Wesley saw all classes as one: they were sinners who needed divine grace. When this view is pursued with vigor, it dissolves the usual divisions between classes. Moreover, in his evangelism Wesley had a particular concern for the poor. His preachers and agents were to go not simply to those who needed them but to those who needed them most. Such an attitude reaps a deep sympathy for the marginalized and destitute of the world. Also, Wesley in his pastoral care gave scope for working-class leadership to develop. In the class meetings, for example, every tenth or twelfth person was a leader by definition. People who had no hope of developing their skills or abilities found scope within a covenanted community to grow far beyond anything that would otherwise be possible. It is small wonder that Wesley continues to cut across racial and national boundaries in his appeal today. Blacks seeking equality, the poor and oppressed seeking liberation, both of these still find inspiration in what he achieved, limited though it was in both thought and practice. He offers a holistic vision of Christian witness.

The Importance of Piety

The sixth strand is rooted in the fascinating spirituality Wesley built into his evangelistic endeavors. This stems in part from his awareness of evil in the world. There is a penetrating realism in his account of human nature that is still very attractive. Many have found in Wesley and the tradition that stems from him an emphasis on sin that matches the violent world they live in and speaks to the facts of their own personal lives. Here he was, of course, within a hair's breadth of Calvinism, and so perhaps should we be if we are to take scripture and experience seriously.

However, for Wesley, where sin abounds, grace much more abounds. God has provided specific and realistic measures for transforming us from sinners into saints. The good news of the gospel is that God's own Son died to make this possible. Yet this past act of grace must never be divorced from the prevenient grace, which comes before to melt our stubborn hearts and bring us to repentance and to our true Father, and from the postvenient grace that sustains us on our pilgrimage to perfect love. In the latter context, Wesley insisted on the indispensability of preaching, prayer, fellowship, the great tradition of the church, Bible reading, meditation on the lives of saints, attendance at the sacraments, peer discipline, testimony, and so on. Grace is never identical with these but it is never divorced from them either. God comes to us through natural means, culminating in his very special presence in the natural gifts of bread and wine at the Lord's supper.

Grace is abundant and yet it is never cheap. It calls for radical repentance and uncompromising commitment to God. Wesley astutely noticed that the latter often involves a critical turning point when the believer quite consciously examines his or her life before yielding it in love to God. His views of sanctification and the annual covenant service, which is one of the great treasures of Methodist liturgy, are fascinating attempts to make theological and practical sense of this insight. But even then, the ultimate focus is not on human decisions or actions, for these are swallowed up in the life of the Spirit, who makes possible the glorious reign of God on earth. The God-centered optimism that finally triumphs in his thought is exhilarating and alluring.

A Catholic Spirit

The last strand that deserves mention is Wesley's emphasis on the catholic spirit. In the sermon of this title he defines this as catholic or universal love. It is love for God and for all humankind, especially for fellow Christians. Wherever it is found, it drives out all forms of bigotry and sectarianism. This love is not blind to differences between people, nor is it indifferent about truth. It is a spirit that respects those who disagree with us or oppose us and provokes all to love each other and do good works.

Wesley's emphasis expressed itself historically in ways that are exasperating to many evangelicals down to this day. Thus it led Wesley to set no theological standards for membership in the Methodist societies. The only condition required was that one desired to flee from the wrath to come. Even where Wesley did impose standards, they were deliberately imprecise. He did not always provide the kind of detailed creed or list of fundamentals that could be used legalistically. He simply left a canonical body of literature, which includes his standard forty-four sermons and his *Notes on the New Testament*. These were not intended to impose a system of formal or speculative theology but to set up standards of preaching and belief that would

secure loyalty to the fundamental truths of the gospel and ensure the continued witness of the church to the realities of the
Christian experience of salvation. This is a far cry from the five
points of Calvinism or of fundamentalism.

The catholic spirit is also reflected in his attitude toward the
Roman Catholic Church in a way that was novel in his day.
Putting it into practice can still be a costly affair in parts of the
modern world. Wesley's *Letter to a Roman Catholic* is justly famous as a worthy piece of ecumenical theology.[14] What is perhaps even more revolutionary was his boldness in calling into
quesiton the nineteenth article of the Church of England because
it cannot accommodate the Roman Catholic Church as part of the
church catholic. That article defines the church as follows:

The visible Church of Christ is a congregation of faithful men, in
which the pure Word of God is preached, and the sacraments be duly
administered.[15]

Wesley's comment speaks for itself.

I will not undertake to defend the accuracy of this definition. I dare not
exclude from the Church catholic all those congregations in which any
unscriptural doctrines which cannot be affirmed to be "the pure Word
of God" are sometimes, yea, frequently preached; neither all those
congregations in which the sacraments are not "duly administered."
Certainly if these things are so, the Church of Rome is not so much a
part of the catholic Church, seeing therein neither is "the pure Word
of God" preached, nor the sacraments "duly administered." Whoever
they are that have "one Spirit, one hope, one Lord, one faith, one God
and Father of all," I can easily bear with their holding wrong opinions,
yea, and superstitious modes of worship. Nor would I, on these accounts, scruple still to include them within the pale of the catholic
Church; neither would I have any objection to receive them, if they
desired it, as members of the Church of England.[16]

It is not surprising, therefore, that Wesley could commend the
Roman Catholic Church for its concern for holiness, and he
gladly gleaned inspiration from its saints. At the same time he
was not afraid to call into question its beliefs and practices

where he felt these perverted the truth of the gospel. The catholic spirit was not an escape from plain speaking and searching honesty when the occasion demanded it.

Conclusion

Where does this analysis of Wesley's legacy leave us? Wesley's significance as a theologian rests fundamentally on his ability to hold together elements in the Christian tradition that generally are pulled apart and expressed in isolation. Thus he integrates contrasting emphases that are vital to a healthy and comprehensive vision of the Christian faith.

Consider the following disjunctive pairs: faith, works; personal devotions, sacramental practice; personal piety, social concern; justification, sanctification; evangelism, Christian nurture; Bible, tradition; revelation, reason; commitment, civility; creation, redemption; cell group, institutional church; local scene, world parish. Very few in the history of the church have been able to live so well with the tensions such partners generate; Wesley was certainly one of these few. For this reason alone, he deserves to be read and pondered.

Moreover, it means that Wesley cannot be tamed by placing him in the categories of the fundamentalist paradigm. Those who look to him as a leader in the Christian faith must insist on this. There are theological riches here that are different from fundamentalism and an embarrassment to no one; we must continue to use them. Those riches extend into the two hundred years of thought and activity within the institutions and traditions he initiated or inspired. Although it is not generally known, that legacy is as rich and substantive as that left to us by Luther and Calvin.[17] That too should make evangelicals think long and hard about what Wesley has to teach us.

6. Revising Evangelical Self-Understanding

At this stage in the discussion, readers might ask what Wesley has to teach us today about any future expression of the evangelical tradition. Modern evangelicals will especially want to ascertain the theological implications of the Wesleyan model. For example, they will be keen to know how the Wesleyan quadrilateral provides a more satisfactory account of biblical authority than that provided, say, by Warfield.

This is a fair request, but it is premature to press for this just now for several reasons. First, it reveals that we have not taken the measure of the Wesleyan version of the tradition. It we proceed in this fashion, Wesley is being used to keep the priorities of the modern experiment intact and secure as before. Wesley has his own peculiar account of authority, which may or may not be correct. To focus on that, however, completely misses the challenge he poses for the modern experiment. That challenge involves relegating the issue of authority to a lower rank on our scale of values. Wesley would have us focus more on the material content of the gospel and its appropriation in life and less on some grand theory of authority supposedly setting a hedge around the faith.

Second, to expect at this stage to be given neat answers to the issue of authority, or for that matter to the other theological issues Wesley raises, is to seek to heal our wounds too quickly. We are once again looking for a hasty panacea that will suddenly set everything right. Such is not to be had, not even from Wesley. For one thing, Wesley is not infallible, hence his views, like those of other models, will have to be evaluated rigorously and comprehensively. For another, Wesley is fundamentally a precritical figure, so it is naive to think that his ideas will necessarily satisfy in a postcritical era. Furthermore, there is no point in pressing the implications of Wesley's ideas or seeking to express them afresh in our own day unless we take Wesley seriously as an alternative model of the evangelical tradition.

At present, the standard self-understanding of the tradition fails to acknowledge this fact. Within that self-understanding, Wesley is generally ignored as a representative of the tradition. Where he is acknowledged, he is construed in one of two ways. He is seen as one more historic exponent of the modern experiment who was a brilliant organizer and evangelist but not a serious theologian. Or he is viewed as a dangerous figure who was committed to an Arminian theology that had liberal tendencies buried deep within it. Adherents of both these interpretations share a common fallacy about the evangelical tradition. They assume that the tradition is uncontested in character. They believe that the evangelical tradition consists in a primitive list of doctrinal essentials that limit the boundaries of the tradition. There is no deep sense that there are alternative, competing accounts of the heritage. Hence the whole ethos and atmosphere of debate within the tradition is polluted. It is riven with pessimism, nervous anxiety, and fear. Fresh suggestions are tested not for their adequacy but for their heretical content, measured by the yardstick of much of the fundamentalist orthodoxy of the recent past. Until we develop a richer account of the tradition, the present impasse will continue.

Evangelicals need initially, therefore, to reflect on the problem Wesley poses simply by being different from the modern experiment. In this chapter I do this in order to offer a more adequate account of the tradition as a whole. I show we can better understand both the unity and diversity of evangelicalism. Through this we can attain much greater self-understanding, something that in time should alter the whole climate of discussion.

The Problem of Unity and Diversity

Let us begin by noting afresh the threat Wesley poses for any definition of the tradition. On the one hand, Wesley is neither a fundamentalist nor a modern conservative evangelical. Thus he differs radically from recent versions of the evangelical tradition. Equally, he differs in key respects from both Calvin and Luther, earlier models of the tradition. On the other hand, Wesley is an evangelical. It is strained to interpret him as a liberal or a Thomist or a Barthian. In fact, Wesley led the evangelical awakening of the eighteenth century. But how then are we to construe the internal content of the tradition? How can we develop an account of the evangelical heritage that can accommodate such diverse figures as Luther, Calvin, Wesley, Warfield, and Henry? Can we meaningfully speak any longer of a single tradition? Can we still insist that there is integrity to the tradition as a whole? Is there still unity in the midst of diversity?

One way to resolve this dilemma is to reject Wesley from the evangelical canon, redrawing the boundaries to exclude him. This is unsatisfactory in the extreme. Wesley cannot be dislodged from the evangelical canon by the stroke of a pen. His position historically is utterly secure. Whatever evangelicalism is, Wesley exemplifies it par excellence. To remove him at this point would be purely arbitrary.

Another way to resolve this dilemma is to turn the first solution around and use Wesley as the exclusive model of the tradition and redraw the boundaries in his favor. Thus figures like Luther, Calvin, Warfield, and Henry are excluded from the tradition by definition. This is equally unsatisfactory, for figures like Luther and Calvin are also constitutive of the tradition. Removing them would be entirely ad hoc at this point in history.

A third solution would be to abandon any notion of a single tradition by insisting that what we have historically is a group of separate traditions that have been mistakenly construed as one. Hence we should abandon any attempt to hold together the unity and diversity of the past. Indeed, in this view, it is misleading to speak of unity. There is no essential unity within the tradition when it is examined historically. It just so happens that the one word "evangelical" was used to refer to contradictory constellations of Christian thought and practice. Thus it would be conceptually more helpful and historically more honest to cease fussing about the internal integrity of the tradition as a whole. Let the modern experiment continue to fall apart theologically and let us wait to see what will arise from the ashes.

This is a drastic solution and one to which I am readily drawn. I reject it, however, for two reasons. First, this solution exacerbates the present tensions within evangelicalism in an unproductive fashion. We surely need to handle the differences and tensions more creatively in the hope that different kinds of evangelicals can provoke one another to revise their own versions of the tradition in an optimum fashion. Second, this solution, although professing conceptual clarity, does not really achieve that goal. It fails to reckon with the unity that does exist. It does not adequately cope with the internal complexity of the tradition and thus really accommodate the unity and diversity that actually exist. Much greater conceptual clarity is possible if we take the time to achieve it. It can be found by acknowledging the contested character of any living tradition. Let me explain what this means.

The Contested Character of the Evangelical Tradition

Consider what we are doing when we use labels to identify a tradition. Often we use them purely descriptively or referentially; we employ them to map complex, dynamic phenomena. Think how difficult it would be to understand the history of philosophy without such concepts as the Enlightenment, Romanticism, empiricism, rationalism, logical positivism, existentialism, and the like. It would be equally impossible to understand the history of the church without such concepts as Roman Catholicism, Eastern Orthodoxy, Protestantism, Methodism, Thomism, and so on. Labels are often used in a relatively neutral, descriptive manner, and the careful thinker will use them without apology and hesitation.

However, we also use religious labels more existentially and prescriptively, especially when we use them to express religious commitment. When people say that they are liberal Protestant, Calvinist, Barthian, evangelical, or whatever, they are identifying the religious tradition that expresses for them who they are, what they believe, and how they relate to the world. They are announcing to the world where they stand; they are sending out signals indicating what action one may expect to encounter from them. To be sure, it is very easy for the signals to be misread. Furthermore, given the predilection humans have for pugnacity and misrepresentation, we can well understand why many want to twist religious labels and use them in their religious warfare. But once we get over this, sensitive insiders can use religious labels to identify quite deliberately some of the convictions and ideals, some of the roles and policies of action they want to embrace and practice. This is no meager achievement, for we all know how difficult it can be to sustain our commitment amidst the varied internal and external pressures that befall us. In times of weakness and stress there is enormous value in drawing on the moral and spiritual resources that a great heritage of thought and action provides. It is good to feel the cheering and encouragement of the great cloud of witnesses who stand in the wings of history behind us.

Precisely because labels are used in this way, it is impossible to reach full agreement on their descriptive content. Different people give diverse accounts of what the essence of the tradition truly is. As W. B. Gallie shows, labels become at that point essentially contested concepts.

The term "essentially contested concept" is a technical one introduced by Gallie to describe certain organized or semi-organized human activities.[1] An important feature of these concepts is that various groups use them in different ways; there is no single application that can be established as standard or correct. A further point about their use is that they continue to be employed even though their users fully recognize the disparate variety of functions they serve; and each party continues to maintain that their use of the concept is the correct or primary function of the term. Also, each party continues to argue its case with what it claims are convincing arguments. According to Gallie, "essentially contested concepts" are concepts "the proper use of which inevitably involves endless disputes about their proper uses on the part of their users."[2] As a result, these concepts can only be understood by means of an appreciation of their history. This clearly applies to the term "evangelical." My basic thesis is that the term "evangelical" functions as a contested concept; thus it is governed in its use by the logical behavior outlined above.

As we have seen, "evangelical" emerged in contemporary Anglo-American life as a badge of increasing significance. This was partly the result of the work of scholars, partly the result of American presidential elections, and partly the result of theological upheaval within conservative theological groups. That upheaval as reflected in the present study has brought to light alternative conceptions of the evangelical tradition. Thus I have shown that Wesley does not fit the standard conception of the tradition articulated by modern evangelicals like Lindsell and Henry. I suspect that the same could be said for both Luther and Calvin. To construe them as fundamentalists or conservative evangelicals would be equally insensitive, although I have not argued that thesis here. So the term "evangelical" embraces at least three constellations of thought: the Reformation, led by Luther and Calvin, the evangelical revival of the eighteenth century as found, say, in Methodism, and modern conservative evangelicalism. Within these historical movements, the meaning of the word "evangelical" is essentially contested. The term is generally used in a mode of appraisal; it is rarely a purely neutral or descriptive term. It is employed to accredit some kind of achievement generally valued by those who apply the term to themselves. The achievement in mind is internally complex. There is no single essence or one particular condition that captures the achievement concerned or will be agreed on by all evangelicals.

Attempts to bypass this fact are just strained and implausible. Invariably people draw up some kind of list of achievements, all of which are part of a complex story they tell about the evangelical tradition as a whole. Sometimes the list is extremely short, containing only two items, say, emphasis on personal regeneration and a commitment to personal evangelism. Sometimes the list can be as long as sixteen items, as illustrated by Kenneth Kantzer's account of the tradition.[3] Within that range there is plenty of scope for choice.

Further, there is no detailed agreement on the achievements that are implicitly built into the concept by its users. Rival descriptions rank the achievements in a different order. Thus William W. Wells, in his *Welcome to the Family: An Introduction to Evangelical Christianity*, organizes a list different from Kantzer's and by doing so sets up slightly different priorities for the tradition.[4] Wells highlights the unique inspiration of scripture, the personal appropiation of salvation, and the pursuit of holiness as the distinctive elements of evangelicalism. Also, each writer or party using the term leaves the description of the prized achievement relatively vague, for it needs to be fleshed out and modified by the examples chosen to give content to the tradition. There is thus often an element of surprise in the exemplars, which can become extremely important for reform and renewal of the heritage. Donald Dayton's work in highlighting the extent to which evangelicals were involved in social causes a century ago is a good case in point.[5] In my own work analogous discoveries about diversity in the doctrine of inspiration encouraged me to make a fresh theological proposal in this area.[6]

This naturally points up the crucial significance of historic exemplars from whom a particular application of the term "evangelical" is derived. The historic exemplars shape the various criteria of achievement and their use. Wesleyans tend to stress the primacy of conversion and spirituality, Calvinists the primacy of correct doctrine. Yet both sides agree that in any accurate account of the evangelical heritage both John Wesley and John Calvin must be included.

The boundaries of these exemplars are never precise. David Alan Hubbard mentions at least seven strands that have a place in the historic succession of evangelicalism, most of which can be plausibly traced back to the influence of notable figures scattered across the world over several centuries.[7] At present there is increasing pressure to see Karl Barth as part of the evangelical succession moving back through Wesley, Calvin, and Luther to Augustine and Paul. In this context it is of interest to note that Donald Bloesch's two volumes, *Essentials of Evangelical Theology*, have more references to Barth than they do to either Luther or Calvin.[8] This move is extremely disturbing to those who look to the American fundamentalists of the early twentieth century as their paradigm for the evangelical heritage. But this should not surprise us in the least. For a long time many reformed evangelicals have but grudgingly accepted that Wesley is of any significance, and Arminius has had an even worse reception.[9] What matters, however, is that despite such disputes, there is relative agreement about the historic exemplars of the tradition. It is not easy to dislodge them from the heart of the heritage, for they are constitutive of the tradition as a whole.

Surprisingly, disputes about the exemplars and their place in the heritage are extremely important. Such disputes keep alive the achievement of these great figures in the history of the church. Indeed they develop their contribution to the people of God in optimum fashion. Exploration of their work, which participation in dispute demands, ensures that they are remembered and that the implications of their ideas and ideals are extended and scrutinized. Of course evangelicals can never consider these exemplars beyond criticism or reproach. They must always be seen as fallible and must be judged in the light of both divine revelation and the best information available in the present. But this critical or sifting process is itself partially inspired and enriched by the disputes they generate among those who look to them as models of the heritage.

Note that it is never possible to predict fully how the heritage will develop as it spreads through space and time. Being human and fallible, this or that part of the tradition may have to be rejected or revised. In addition, new discoveries about the world or about human nature have to be assimilated, and new insights about the interpretation of scripture need to be appropriated, and new methods of biblical study have to be absorbed. Developments in society and culture raise fresh questions whose answers call for a change of emphasis or tone. In these and varied ways, subtle transformations take place unawares. Even opposition to developments in, say, science or biblical studies may alter the character of the tradition in ways unimaginable beforehand.

It can readily be seen, then, that the term "evangelical" is an essentially contested concept. There is necessarily a prolonged and intense dispute about its nature. The implications of this are far-reaching for evangelicals, as we shall see shortly. For the moment let me state the central point of this chapter by means of an analogy.

The Contest Illustrated

Becoming an evangelical is not unlike joining a first-division soccer team. To get into the league at all your team must meet certain basic requirements. There must be eleven players; there must be an adequate defense; there must be mid-field strategists who can control the flow of play; there must be the ability to score goals regularly. The evangelical tradition is similar. To join it, you must satisfy certain minimal conditions. You must, for example, be "born again," you must be committed to evangelism, you must believe in the substance of the orthodox creeds, you must hold to the authority of scripture, and so on. These essentials secure the internal integrity of the tradition.

These set the minimum standard for entry into the tradition. Yet the list is not absolutely final or settled forever. All that we can hope for is partial and relative agreement about the essentials of the tradition.

Moreover, within the league, the various teams measure up to these standards in different ways. Some are stronger in defense than in offense. Some have more star players than others. And each team can look back to great players of the past who shine as great lights in the world of soccer. Also, there are recognizably distinct styles of play; managers and coaches have different ways of organizing the team on the field. While on the field, game plans have to be changed in the light of weather conditions and the opposing team. After all, improvisation and development are vital for the health and success of any team. Yet over time characteristic features develop and readily come to mind when supporters speak of the greatness of their team.

Likewise, within the evangelical tradition certain expressions of the heritage are stronger in some areas than in others. The Salvation Army shines in social involvement; Calvinists constantly remind us of the sovereign greatness of God; Wesleyans put strong store by spiritual formation. Various strands of the tradition produce over time outstanding exponents of their unique ways of interpreting the riches of the faith and each will look to great figures of the past to act as paradigms of the heritage. These figures vary in different strands of the tradition, so that a paradigm for one group does not necessarily act as a paradigm for another. Indeed there is intense rivalry as to which group has the best paradigm and this spills over into endless dispute as to how best to express the heritage. However, responsible and sensible adherents of each side in this contest always recognize the legitimacy of the opponents ideals, partly because there is no way they can publicly prove that their own ideals are better.

As there are no cup finals or league matches to settle objectively who is best, these disputes have an air of unreality about them at times. Yet their existence keeps people thinking about the importance of the game and prompts them to reflect more creatively on how to play it. Moreover, as there are no clear-cut boundaries to the evangelical league, it is, on the surface, relatively easy for one team to claim that another team does not really belong in the first division. Some even try and argue that the other team is not playing soccer but some other game: they insist that they have taken to playing rugby or hockey. In such circumstances it is difficult to work together for the reform of the game or, for that matter, to spread it to other parts of the world.

At times pitched battles take place between rival gangs of supporters. Even managers and star players are known to loose their tempers and join in. In the heat of the contest it is easy to become overconfident about the correctness of one's team and blind to the merits of one's rivals. It is always dangerous when this happens, for the league as a whole is liable to be brought into disrepute and then people and players must look to another league for fulfillment.

In all this the best teams are those that have cultivated the most creative traditions and have nourished their whole range of players from goal keeper to forwards. In new worlds stability and flexibility are at a premium. To play in the world league, teams must be able to adapt to changed conditions both within and without. There can be no standing still. Yet it must be the same game that they play and they must play it with style and flair. The challenge to contemporary evangelicals at this point is both awesome and exciting. They are more likely to measure up to it if they will face squarely the implications of this analysis. Before exploring these, let us note briefly a linguistic prejudice that must be overcome if the revised self-understanding of the tradition is to be accepted.

A Concluding Caution

One of the reasons why evangelicals fail to acknowledge the diversity within the evangelical past stems from a passion for precise, clear-cut definitions. They are deeply suspicious of concepts that cannot be specified in an objective, agreed upon fashion. This is undoubtedly one reason why they cling to the concept of inerrancy and spend so much time trying to finalize a definition of it once and for all. This point is well expressed by Carl F. H. Henry in his rejection of Clark Pinnock's call to play down the significance of the concept.

Pinnock's objections to the term inerrancy are . . . unpersuasive. All terms require strict definition, terms like infallibility and inspiration no less than inerrancy. If the possibility of misunderstanding becomes all-decisive for our choice of words, we would need to remain speechless.[10]

This is a revealing comment. It indicates very clearly that modern evangelicals will be uneasy with my call for much greater sensitivity in understanding the tradition. Not only does that call challenge the historic prejudice that ignores the complex inner dynamics of the past, it also cuts across the desire for strict definition. I am proposing that we make a virtue of our failure to reach agreement on the essentials of evangelicalism. Most evangelicals, if they follow Henry in his strictures about language, will find this puzzling in the extreme.

7. Altering the Climate of Debate

Anyone who has experienced the frustration accompanying attempts to define evangelicalism in a univocal way will welcome the revised understanding of the heritage presented above. The tradition is a contested tradition. There are competing ways of outlining and organizing its internal structure and emphasis. These differ quite radically from one another, so we must abandon the drive, so characteristic of recent years, to squeeze the great historic exemplars of the past into the revised mold of modern fundamentalism. Yet there is still integrity to the heritage. The word "evangelical" is not so Pickwickian that it can be used to refer to any version of the Christian tradition. Evangelicals are committed to a set of incomplete yet definite convictions. They also agree, more or less, on the constitutive exemplars of the tradition. Hence evangelicalism can be distinguished from such other well-known versions of the Christian tradition as liberalism, Anglo-Catholicism, Thomism, or fundamentalism. It is there whether we like it or not; it has its own integrity; and it should be taken seriously as an honorable account of the Christian faith.

If the evangelical tradition is a contested tradition, then this has crucial implications for the texture of debate within evangelicalism, within the church at large, and within scholarly circles. In this chapter I focus mostly on the implications for evangelicals. My analysis calls for a change in the climate of debate. As I explore this I shall inevitably be entering into the contest as to how best to express the tradition in the future.

Treating Tensions Positively

One of the first things evangelicals must do is to learn to take full advantage of their divisions. Conflict and tension need not be destructive; they are a vital part of a healthy heritage. Disagreement over emphasis, differences about theological detail, variance in ethical stance, these should spur all concerned to express their own positions as clearly and rigorously as possible. Provided there is broad agreement about the general principles and convictions of the tradition, conflict should be creatively used to bring out the best in everyone. Tension can contribute positively to the welfare of all.

Evangelicals, therefore, should stop complaining about the lack of agreement among themselves. Recently, for example, Robert K. Johnston in his *Evangelicals at an Impasse*[1] laments at length the absence of agreement on such matters as the role of women, social ethics, and homosexuality. He expresses his concern at the outset.

Beyond my desire to address specific theological issues and to suggest directions in which evangelicals might profitably move, I have attempted to give voice in this book to a more basic and persistent concern. That evangelicals, all claiming a common Biblical norm, are reaching contradictory theological formulations on many of the major issues they are addressing suggests the problematic nature of their present understanding of theological interpretation. To argue that the Bible is authoritative, but to be unable to come to anything like agreement on what it says (even with those who share an evangelical commitment), is self-defeating. It is this belief which has served as an organizing principle in my writing.[2]

Johnston is undoubtedly accurate in what he writes about diversity. The mistake is in his expectations. The kind of unity he seeks has never been attained by evangelicals. Indeed they differ not just on how scripture should be interpreted, they differ on how to construe its authority, not to mention a host of other issues, as Johnston himself acknowledges.[3] To be sure, this creates difficulties for united action on those matters over which there is disagreement. But these will not be resolved by the kind of wishful thinking in which Johnston indulges. Rather, they may never be resolved and as a result the cooperative ventures of evangelicals call for a wholly different perspective on both the issues and the tradition itself. Disagreement may well be the very vice that needs to be transformed into a virtue at this point.

What is ultimately at issue here is tolerance within the tradition itself. One of the unfortunate legacies of fundamentalism is its devout intolerance of those who do not share its diagnosis and solution to the problems of theology and the church. They and their modern evangelical offspring are too quick to dismiss their opponents as heretics. This applies even in the case where the opponent is working out of an alternative strand of the evangelical tradition. This pollutes the whole atmosphere of discussion. Evangelicals must resist such intolerance aggressively; if they do not, then the future looks grim indeed, for modern evangelicalism will degenerate beyond repair. The creative forces essential to new life and expression will either go underground or disappear entirely.

At present this constitutes one of the greatest threats to the tradition as a whole. There is an atmosphere of pessimism abroad dampening the fires of enthusiasm. Many see the present upheaval as a threat to the heritage rather than the natural end of an era. There is a loss of excitement about the great heroes of the past. There is no sense that the future is genuinely open and that God may well desire to renew the world in a profoundly new way, bringing forth through the inspiration of the Holy Spirit new expressions of the evangelical tradition. If this is to happen, then we should seek generously to encourage those who are attempting to articulate and express the tradition today. At present the atmosphere is one of gloom and doom and it stems in part from a narrow self-understanding of what the heritage has been over the years. If evangelicals could acknowledge the contested character of the tradition, then this trend could be radically reversed. Tensions and conflict could be used creatively to renew the tradition for future generations.

The Debate About Inerrancy

It is from this vantage point that we should view the present heated debate about the Bible initiated by Harold Lindsell.[4] Evangelicals owe a great debt to Lindsell, for he confirms a point made years ago by E. J. Carnell, who noted that the dialogue on inspiration between James Orr and the Princeton theologians was never successfully terminated.[5] The debate went underground, the fountain of ideas dried up, the conversation on the issue stopped and, "as a result, a heavy pall of fear hangs over the academic community. When a gifted professor tries to interact with the critical difficulties in the text, he is charged with disaffection, if not outright heresy."[6] Lindsell clearly brings this matter right out in the open for all to see. For this we should all be grateful.

What is not a gain is the way in which the debate is conducted. At this level Lindsell is a poor contestant, for he will not acknowledge that those who reject inerrancy can be part of the tradition. What he presupposes is a narrow and exclusivist interpretation of the heritage. Like many fundamentalist evangelicals, Lindsell is working with a rigidly defined account of evangelicalism, within which inerrancy is the litmus test of authenticity. In itself this reflects the thoroughly rationalistic, deductivist character of the fundamentalist mentality, which rests on enormous confidence in our ability to package and present theological truth neatly and once and for all. Such a mentality is very uneasy with less precise, more fluid, more developmental concepts.

Now if Lindsell were merely arguing for his own position on inerrancy, while recognizing that it was likely to be contested by fellow evangelicals, there would be nothing to quarrel with strategically. What Lindsell and his colleagues have done is set the debate in a false and misleading context. That context needs to be radically altered by a full and daring acknowledgment that the tradition really is contested. The debate needs to take place in a context where it is already granted that the concept of evangelicalism cannot be defined in a strict, take-it-or-leave-it manner. Thereby the whole character of the debate will be lifted to an entirely different level. As it stands, Lindsell is unable to recognize that his opponents may themselves quite legitimately lay claim to being evangelicals. As a result, any real debate or meeting of minds is almost impossible from the outset. Unless there is a conscious awareness of the contested character of the term "evangelical," it is unlikely that any debate will take place; the probable outcome of a continued impasse is a serious fragmentation of the evangelical tradition in our day.

Contrast this with what might happen were the contested character of the concept to be acknowledged. The quality of the debate could be drastically improved. Gallie expresses this succinctly.

Recognition of a given concept as essentially contested implies recognition of rival uses of it (such as oneself repudiates) as not only logically possible and humanely "likely," but as of permanent potential critical value to one's own use or interpretation of the concept in question; whereas to regard any rival use as anathema, perverse, bestial or lunatic means, in many cases, to submit oneself to the chronic human peril of underestimating, or of completely ignoring, the value of one's opponents' positions. One desirable consequence of the required recognition in any proper instance of essential contestedness might therefore be a marked raising of the level of quality of arguments in the disputes of the contestant parties. And this would mean, *prima facie,* a justification of the continued competition for support and acknowledgement between the various contesting parties.[7]

Once all sides acknowledge that their own position about inerrancy will be contested by others who can claim equal loyalty to the gospel, to Christ, and to the evangelical heritage, then the real issues can be faced courageously and critically.

I myself would argue that inerrancy is both inadequate and

dangerous as a predicate of scripture. It stems historically from a doctrine of dictation, which evangelicals themselves have rejected. It creates enormous difficulties no one has satisfactorily resolved. It inhibits an honest reading of the text, as it is, blemishes and all. It fosters an obsession with epistemological questions that overshadows the substance of the gospel. It creates expectations in young converts that can never be fulfilled and then proceeds to provide circuitous harmonizations and theories to relieve the ensuing disappointment. It is not based on scripture itself, it is ultimately irreconcilable with the actual phenomena of the Bible, and it is not required for construing scripture as normative for Christian faith and practice.

Lindsell and others hold a contrary view. They believe that inerrancy is a proper inference from inspiration. They hold that it is essential to a consistent view of authority, that without it anything goes in theology, and that rejecting it is the beginning of a slippery slope leading to atheism. They insist that all evangelicals have held to inerrancy, that it is an essential bulwark against improper study of the Bible, and that the difficulties it generates are cosmetic in character. So be it. There is a genuine argument here of obvious importance. Moreover, it is clear that these issues are self-involving, for all sides believe that they have an impact, positively or negatively, on the welfare of the faithful. However, there is no monopoly of concern about the well-being of the church. Hence let all sides argue their case without misrepresentation and accusations of betrayal or disloyalty. Let there be a genuine tolerance of contrasting positions within the one contested tradition.

Improving External Relations

We can expand this appeal for tolerance to include a much more respectful and less defensive attitude to other Christian traditions. This can be generated by noting that not only the evangelical tradition but the Christian tradition as a whole is contested in character. Rather than excommunicating other

Christians from the kingdom, evangelicals should use the existing differences to go back into their corners, to review their own position, and then to out-think and out-love their opponents. Wesley was forced to do this when confronted by Calvinists; it made him think through afresh the doctrine of predestination and attempt to improve on the alternatives. Likewise evangelicals, both Wesleyan and Calvinist, when confronted with genuine liberals, should think first not of charges of heresy but of articulating more carefully their own position. The conflict should be a spur for improvement, not an excuse for ranting about liberalism. Unfortunately, evangelicals too readily use their commitment to evangelical orthodoxy as an apologetic device to dodge the real issues.

Consider, for example, the strategy adopted by Gresham Machen in his broadside against liberal theology, *Christianity and Liberalism*.[9] No less a figure than Walter Lippman rated this as the best popular argument produced in the fundamentalist–modernist controversy.[10] Lippman was especially pleased with the cool, calm, and collected clarity that is a mark of Machen's writing. I have enormous sympathy with this assessment, for the book is in some respects a delight to read. What is unfortunate, however, is the level at which the argument is developed. Consider the following statement of his aim:

Modern liberalism may be criticised (1) on the ground that it is un-Christian and (2) on the ground that it is unscientific. We shall concern ourselves here chiefly with the former line of criticism; we shall be interested in showing that despite the liberal use of traditional phraseology modern liberalism not only is a different religion from Christianity but belongs in a totally different class of religions.[11]

Machen's primary aim is to show that liberalism does not measure up to Machen's own definition of orthodoxy. Thus he proceeds to set out the liberal's position on God, humanity, the Bible, and so forth, showing in turn that they fall short of his standards. This is a rather futile exercise. Not only does it ignore the contested character of the Christian tradition as a whole, but it also presupposes that liberalism is a monolithic tradition that can be specified without much difficulty. Not only does it not seek to appropriate the positive insights that liberal Christians have to share with other Christians, but it also fails to come to terms with the key problems that gave rise to liberal Christianity in the first place. It is not surprising, therefore, that those contemporary evangelicals who look to figures like Machen as their models still have not really addressed the questions raised by such great liberals as Ernst Troeltsch, and even Schleiermacher himself, in any fundamental way. Their masters have done a surprisingly good job in initiating them into a form of evangelicalism that continues to sidestep the modern world.

Undoubtedly one reason for this state of affairs stems from fear. Modern evangelicals have a great fear of anything coming from the Enlightenment. To be sure, it can be argued that there is much in the Enlightenment and its aftermath that should be rejected. For example, it has undoubtedly bequeathed to us the popular view that sees science as the answer to everything. This is an impoverished mentality we are wise to reject. But even then, we must be careful. Secularism is a serious option in the modern world, which has its able and responsible defenders within modern philosophy. It will not be outwitted or outthought by those who reject it disdainfully and uncritically. In any case, fearing it helps no one. Indeed nervousness betrays a shallow commitment to divine providence. It implies that God has abandoned creation to unbelief to a degree last held by the deists of the eighteenth century. Besides, fear casts out love and therefore it ruins any hope of exercising a catholic spirit toward those outside the faith.

Evangelicals cannot profess to love and respect their opponents in scholarly circles if they fail to take seriously the alternative proposals and competing arguments they present. Evangelicals must extend to their intellectual adversaries the minimum courtesy of a fair hearing and a considered response. Recognizing the contested and controversial character of religious and metaphysical issues would bring closer the dawn of a new day when opposing positions would be considered on their merits rather than on their orthodoxy or their heterodoxy.

This does not mean that we should abandon the concept of heresy within the church. There are views that are clearly incompatible with the gospel of Christ and Christians have a duty to guard the faith once delivered to the saints. However, in applying the concept at least two things should be borne in mind. First, the concept of heresy is of little or no value in critically assessing a position within modern scholarship. To call a position heretical is to claim that it is incompatible with a proper conception of the Christian faith. However, in the world of scholarship, the debate ultimately proceeds to a level where the issue of what a proper conception of the Christian faith in fact is, is itself an issue. Referring to a particular creed as heretical does not settle that issue; it simply begs the question in advance. Secondly, the concept of heresy is fundamentally an ecclesiastical concept used by a particular group to safeguard its doctrinal integrity and purity. It clearly may have to be invoked in times of crisis and apostasy as a serious warning, as happened in Germany in the thirties when the Nazis threatened the essence of the gospel. It requires great spiritual and moral sensitivity to know when such moments occur. Evangelicals, however, tend to use the concept much too readily and incautiously. As a result, they discredit its employments and exaggerate their own doctrinal purity. To redress the balance, evangelicals need to become much more aware of the danger of heresy within groups where they least expect it. In my view, those groups who now speak of the divinity and humanity of the Bible have clearly become heretical. Unfortunately most evangelicals are themselves so obsessed with scripture that they fail to recognize this.

Celebrating Our Humanity

I fully acknowledge that it will not be easy for many evangelicals to make the changes I am proposing. It will mean owning up more honestly to the fragility and complexity of the human condition. Evangelicals have placed so much emphasis on divine revelation and original sin that they are almost afraid to be human. Ideas that cannot be traced directly to the Bible are held to be contaminated in a deep way by sin and are therefore to be treated with suspicion. Salvation has been made to depend so crucially upon correct doctrine that human interests other than religious interests are often seen as dangerous to the soul. Because there has been little sense of evangelicalism as a tradition, modern evangelicals have no awareness of the fallibility of their own proposals. To question the evangelical position has been to question God and risk one's eternal salvation. Such an atmosphere is spiritually and intellectually suffocating. It is surely essential to human maturity that there be genuine freedom; freedom, in turn, cannot be exercised where there is no appreciation for the fragility, the complexity, the richness, and the ambiguity of the human condition. People must be given space to make mistakes and to come to personal maturity within the tradition on their own. Evangelicals need to celebrate the fact that in developing and contesting even their own tradition, they are engaging in a divinely intended human activity. If they do not, then the tradition will become sterile, evangelicals will take themselves far too seriously, and their own children will have to rebel to preserve their humanity.

This is exactly what happened in much of nineteenth-century British evangelicalism. The tradition became so rigid both doctrinally and morally that a younger generation found it impossible to cope with its strictures. It is worth pausing to listen to two witnesses who speak eloquently of this danger.

George Eliot begins a scathing review of the works of Dr. Cumming, an eminent evangelical preacher and author, in the following fashion:

Given a man with moderate intellect, a moral standard not higher than the average, some rhetorical affluence and great glibness of speech, what is the career in which, without the aid of birth of money, he may most easily attain power and reputation in English society? Where is that Goshen of mediocrity in which a smattering of science and learning will pass for profound instruction, where platitudes will be accepted as wisdom, bigoted narrowness as holy zeal, unctuous egoism as God-given piety? Let such a man become an evangelical preacher; he will then find it possible to reconcile such small ability with great ambition, superficial knowledge with prestige of erudition, a middling morale with a high reputation for sanctity. Let him shun practical extremes and be ultra only in what is purely theoretic: let him be stringent on predestination, but latitudinarian on fasting; unflinching in insisting on the Eternity of punishment, but diffident of curtailing the substantial comforts of time; ardent and imaginative on the pre-millennial advent of Christ, but cold and cautious towards every other infringement of the status quo. Let him fish for souls not with the bait of inconvenient singularity, but with the dragnet of comfortable conformity. Let him be hard and literal in his interpretation only when he wants to hurl texts at the heads of unbelievers and adversaries, but when the letter of Scriptures presses too closely on the genteel Christianity of the nineteenth century, let him use his spiritualizing alembic and disperse it into impalpable ether. Let him preach less of Christ than of Anti-Christ; let him be less definite in showing what sin is than in showing who is the Man of Sin, less expansive on the blessedness of faith than on the accursedness of infidelity. Above all let him set up as an interpreter of prophecy, and rival Moore's Almanack in the prediction of political events, tickling the interest of hearers who are but moderately spiritual by showing how the Holy Spirit has dictated problems and charades for their benefit, and how, if they are ingenious enough to solve these, they may have their Christian graces nourished by learning precisely to whom they may point as the "horn that had eyes," "the lying prophet," and the "unclean spirits." In this way he will draw men to him by the strong cords of their passions, made reason-proof by being baptized with the name of piety. In this way he may gain a metropolitan pulpit; the avenues to his church will be crowded as the passages to the opera; he has but to print his prophetic sermons and bind them in lilac and gold, and they will adorn the drawing room table of all evangelical ladies, who will regard as a sort of pious "light reading" the demonstration that the prophesy of the locusts whose sting is in their tail is fulfilled in the fact of the Turkish commander's having taken a horse's tail for his standard, and that the French are the very frogs predicted in the Revelation.[12]

Eliot proceeds to argue that the temperament thus described is not an accident. It is intimately related to an ideology that has lost much of the sensitivity of orthodox theology. That ideology has tended to subvert moral development by imposing upon personal growth an alien system of conceptions and values that has little sympathy for human life as actually created by God. There is no sense within this of the dignity and worth of the human person. This tendency has deep roots in the Calvinistic version of the evangelical tradition.

A similar criticism to that of George Eliot is voiced by Sir Edmund Gosse. Gosse's father was an eminent Victorian zoologist, who was a member of the Plymouth Brethren. Gosse senior is chiefly known for his famous "solution" to the discrepancy between a literal reading of Genesis and the findings of geology. He proposed that God created the world with all the fossils positioned in a plausibly misleading pattern in order to test our faith. His son, Edmund, was early initiated into the evangelical faith of his father. He was publicly baptized at the age of ten, but over the years the tradition proved incapable of meeting his intellectual and aesthetic needs. In the end he broke from it. In later life he turned down the professorship of English literature at Harvard, opting instead for a lectureship at Cambridge. He eventually became librarian to the House of Lords and died in 1928 at the age of seventy-nine. His biography, *Father and Son*,[13] is a poignant account of his pilgrimage. In recounting his break with his father's faith, he pinpoints a persistent danger in evangelical religion.

Let me speak plainly. After my long experience, after my patience and forbearance, I have surely the right to protest against the untruth (would that I could apply to it any other word!) that evangelical religion, or any religion in a violent form, is a wholesome or valuable or desirable adjunct to human life. It divides heart from heart. It sets up a vain, chimerical ideal, in the barren pursuit of which all the tender, indulgent affections, all the genial play of life, all the exquisite pleasures and soft resignations of the body, all that enlarges and calms the soul, are exchanged for what is harsh and void and negative. It encourages a stern and ignorant spirit of condemnation; it throws altogether out of gear the healthy movement of the conscience; it invents virtues which are sterile and cruel; it invents sins which are no sins at all, but which darken the heaven of innocent joy with futile clouds of remorse. There is something horrible, if we bring ourselves to face it, in the fanaticism that can do nothing with this pathetic and fugitive existence of ours but treat it as if it were the uncomfortable antechamber to a palace which no one has explored and of the plan of which we know absolutely nothing. My father, it is true, believed that he was intimately acquainted with the form and furniture of this habitation, and he wished me to think of nothing else but of the advantages of an eternal residence in it.[14]

There is no easy solution to the problem George Eliot and Sir Edmund Gosse highlight here. Surely, however, a sense of the human character of the evangelical experiment would explode the myth that it is a simple transcript of the divine will. It is a serious human attempt to sum up and transmit in viable form the riches of the gospel. It is a thoroughly human enterprise, with all the risks and joys which that enjoins. If evangelicals would accept this, it would at once release them from exaggerating the importance of their own systems of thought and action and thereby liberate them to listen more sensitively to the cry of the human heart within their own borders. They might even begin to celebrate their own humanity as a precious gift from God and thus change the climate of opinion within the tradition as a whole.

Fostering Responsible Forms of Initiation

What I have just argued does not imply that evangelicals should be indifferent about initiating each new generation into specific versions of the heritage. Evangelicals are, in fact, very fortunate to have at their disposal a large range of educational institutions. These are extremely important, especially those at the university level. Evangelical universities not only transmit the heritage, they also make manifest the diversity of the tradition. Because most evangelicals have little sense of the contested character of the tradition, they become impatient with too much diversity. Many would like all evangelical universities and seminaries to be expressions of one single model of the tradition. What we should expect and work for is the reverse of this. We need to foster rival versions of the evangelical tradition, with one university naturally developing, say, the Calvinist version of the heritage, another, say, the Wesleyan version, another, say, the neo-evangelical version. It is crucial that there be centers of learning to examine and articulate, and thereby keep alive, the memory of those who have represented the best of the evangelical past. It is quite wrong to think that such institutions have to be sectarian in character. On the contrary, if one recognizes the contested character of the evangelical faith, then sectarianism will automatically be rejected.

At whatever level the tradition is transmitted, whether in the home or in the church or in the university, it is pivotal that responsible forms of initiation be adopted. What is needed is the striking of a fine balance between authoritarianism and permissivism. Basil Mitchell, an Oxford philospher, provides exactly the advice evangelicals should heed.

The process of being educated is like learning to build a house by actually building one and then having to live in the house one has built. It is a process in which the indvidual inevitably requires help. The extreme authoritarian helps by building the house himself according to what he believes to be the best plan and making the novice to live in it. He designs it in such a way as to make it as difficult as possible for the novice to alter it. The extreme liberal leaves the novice to find his own materials and devise his own plan, for fear of exercising improper influence. The most he will do is provide strictly technical information if asked. The sensible educator helps the novice to build the best house he can (in the light of accumulated experience). He strikes a balance between the need to produce a good house and the desirability of letting the novice make his own choices; but he is careful that the house is designed in such a way that it can subsequently be altered and improved as the owner, no longer a novice, sees fit.[15]

The evangelical tradition will no doubt continue to produce its fair share of authoritarian educators who ride roughshod over the hearts and minds of those souls under their care. I have heard some evangelicals confess that they were first respected as individuals only when they went to graduate schools in leading "liberal" institutions. This is a severe indictment of some forms of the tradition. It would be naive to believe that they will be reformed or sanctified overnight. However, the large number of evangelicals who are emerging from the heritage to pursue the theological task with humility and rigor and the coming of age of some of the evangelical institutions of higher education in America are welcome signs of change. Acknowledging the contested character of the tradition will foster the kind of climate in which further changes can be attempted and critically examined.

The Attitude of Outsiders

The process of change could be greatly enhanced were outsiders to develop a more penetrating account of the evangelical position. Few outsiders are aware of the theological character of the tradition. It has been fashionable to dismiss evangelicals by deploying rather crude psychological or sociological explanations of their origins. Thus evangelicals have been pictured as very insecure people in search of some kind of absolute authority to settle decisively the issues perplexing them. There is, of course, some truth in this but it must not be exaggerated. After all, this is a problem by no means peculiar to evangelicals. Many Christians have fled to the arms of mother church to settle everything for them. We should seek to understand this phenomenon rather than belittle it. Alternatively, it has been common to construe evangelicalism as a predominantly rural phenomenon. It has been tempting to see it as a reactionary development, intended to prevent people from adopting or adapting to the ideas and conventions (presumably liberal and dangerous) of the modern world. This overlooks the attraction evangelicalism has had both in the cities and on every level of society. In any case, tracing the psychological and social origins of a movement does not in itself discredit its theological proposals. At some stage these should be explored in their own right and evaluated sympathetically.

Christians outside evangelicalism can easily underestimate the strength and clarity of the evangelical tradition, especially where they identify evangelicals as "fundamentalists with good manners," or where they confuse evangelicalism with fringe activities like camp meetings, antipathy to the cinema, unstructured church services, saccharine gospel songs, right-wing conservative politics, or passionate anti-intellectualism. Such judgments rest on half-baked historical analysis of the phenomena at issue. In the tough and stormy world of ecclesiastical politics, it is always tempting to go for the quick kill by fastening on what is obviously bizarre or obnoxious. As Gallie points out: "Every movement or group or party has its more or less lunatic fringe—fanatics of their own self-righteousness or dyed-in-the-wool gloaters in their exclusive orthodoxy."[16] So long as we focus on such a small sample, verbal victory will always be easy. Such victories, however, rest on extremely shallow analysis of complex historical entities and they are no less shallow when they are advanced by professional historians. Besides, they are essentially sub-Christian in character, for they involve an implicit rejection of a catholic spirit. Even if evangelicals are thoroughly wrong, then other Christians can share in the magnanimous judgment of Paul when he rejoiced that Christ was still being preached by those who did it out of envy and rivalry.[17]

Nothing that I have said here invites opponents of the evangelical tradition to suffer fools gladly or even to hold their fire. Evangelicalism has its problems and its dangers. Other Christians have a duty to explain these honestly, so that the wise may avoid them. Evangelicals, in their turn, should be humble enough to confess their faults and learn from the criticism of others. This is unlikely to happen, if external critics fail to recognize the complex, contested character of the tradition. Moverover, if there has to be theological warfare, let it at least be conducted fairly. Let the targets be identified clearly and correctly, and let the battles be fought with clean and honorable weapons.

8. Provoking Theological Renewal

The present crisis in modern evangelicalism gives it a golden opportunity to put its house in order. We have clearly reached the end of an era. In arriving at that conclusion we have made two important discoveries. First, we have become aware that the experiment of the last generation is but one way of articulating the internal commitments of the heritage. There are other models that capture more fully what the tradition ought to be. Second, we have become acquainted with the contested character of the tradition. The tensions existing within it are a sign of health and vitality. They reveal that serious attempts are being made to renew and revitalize the inheritance bequeathed to us from the past. If we face the implications of these discoveries then we shall revise our understanding of what the tradition is as a whole and, in the light of this, seek to alter the present climate of opinion.

These recommendations apply to all within the evangelical tradition. It does not matter at this stage which version of the tradition one espouses. Diversity and radical tension exist as a matter of historical fact; one must come to terms with them and explore the consequences of them for the future. This applies whether one looks principally to Calvin, to Luther, to Wesley, to Warfield, or to Henry as the model for the tradition. Indeed, one can acknowledge the existence of radical diversity within the tradition without altering one's fundamental theological orientation. One cannot accept it, however, without acknowledging the experimental character of the heritage. Once one realizes that there are different ways of expressing the tradition, then one must acknowledge the relative, human character of the whole enterprise.

This is deeply disturbing, for it means owning up to the mortal and fallible character of the tradition. Most evangelicals are reluctant to do this, for in practice they construe their own position as identical with the truth of God. This is perfectly natural. Evangelicals, like other self-respecting believers, will want to believe the truth, and if they believe in special revelation, they will want to believe the truth revealed by God. They will therefore hold that their position best represents the truth of God. There is nothing odd or reprehensible about this. What is at issue, however, is whether this is actually the case. It is always possible that evangelicals are wrong; they are not infallible. Indeed it would be dogmatic in the extreme to think that there is no room for correction and improvement. Hence evangelicals have a duty to acknowledge the experimental character of their position. All should recognize the contested character of the heritage, revise the present climate of opinion accordingly, and then proceed to provoke one another to love and good works.

Calling All Evangelicals to Action

We should also spur one another on to develop our theological positions as coherently and richly as possible. Thus dissatisfaction with the reigning paradigm or with other models of the tradition should lead neither to excessive complaining about the present nor to helpless nostalgia for the good old days, but to determined effort to provide better expositions of the heritage. Such efforts will run in one of two channels. Either they will involve a penetrating appropriation and development of a past expression of the tradition, or they will involve a wholly new way of developing the major themes and structure of the heritage.

In the former case, one will articulate a fresh account of, say, the Calvinist or Wesleyan version of the Christian faith. One will look to a Wesley or Calvin as a kind of adviser and friend, as one seeks to spell out what it means to be an evangelical Christian in our own day and generation. One will examine carefully the ingredients of their success, without being blind to their weaknesses and mistakes. It is wise, of course, to be acquainted with as many exemplars of the tradition as possible. However, sooner or later one will gravitate toward one particular exemplar, judging that one to be a richer or more adequate expression of the tradition.

It is not for me to tell readers which exemplar to choose. What matters is that we be aware of what we are doing and that we realize the great value of exploring and expressing various versions of the heritage. It is up to evangelicals to find out which edition they consider most healthy and seek to improve upon it as best they can. Even when we have opted for a particular exemplar, we should still keep a watchful eye on developments elsewhere. Opposing accounts of the inheritance can be extremely illuminating both in their strengths and weaknesses. We will almost certainly not like what we behold, but examining the efforts of opponents can be invaluable in identifying where improvements have to be made. Moreover, noting the detailed criticisms of others against our own position is a purifying experience that should prevent us retreating to impregnable ghettos of isolation.

It is true, to be sure, that many evangelicals do not know where they fit on the map of the past. Perhaps none of the great exemplars appeals to them in a unique way. Or perhaps they have moved in and out of various churches and institutions where there have been rival versions of the tradition available. They may feel rootless and confused. Some may even resent the thought that they should identify with any particular expression of the tradition; this seems narrow and restrictive to them.

I have no desire to dictate what such people should do. I think it advisable, however, to examine carefully where one stands. There is no virtue in being an evangelical nomad, wandering aimlessly from one stance to another. Without stable theological commitments, one is liable to be tossed about by every wind of change that blows. Besides, it is much more interesting to play the game rather than lounge on the sidelines as a spectator. Even if one does shop around initially, it is more fruitful to appropriate the rich content of one version of the tradition and see where it leads. There is nothing to lose. On the contrary, the gains are considerable. At the very least the great exemplars of the past function as sources of distant historical inspiration; they exemplify certain standards to which one is naturally committed. They constitute ideals that at once encourage and chasten one's endeavors.

In this process, it is fatal if these models become our masters. To become a slave to any particular model of the tradition is self-defeating and dangerous. If one treats a Calvin or a Wesley as beyond criticism, then one is ignoring both the relativity of the Christian past and the blind spots any great exponent of the heritage inevitably exhibits. More importantly, one is making the scriptures subservient to tradition, a move no evangelical can make without radical inconsistency. Also, one is losing that vital sense of creative independence that is crucial if the spirit of the tradition is to be kept alive over the generations.

It is not easy to strike a correct balance in these matters. In order to avoid slavery, it is very tempting to abandon the past and revolt in the name of personal autonomy, disclaiming any loyalty to past exemplars. This is naive and unrealistic. Even if we reject one version of the Christian past, this does not mean that we will not come under the influence of another. Personal autonomy is a myth that is best forgotten. If we reject, say, a Calvin or Wesley, we will almost certainly find ourselves inspired by some other exemplar or group of exemplars. In any case, we need the enrichment the past provides. If we rebel prematurely, then we are liable to be seduced by the *unconscious* ideals of our own times. We need the inspiration and correctives of the historic landmarks of the tradition to bring us to maturity and to enrich and enliven our judgments as to what is to be retrieved and what is to be rejected for the future.

Knowing this is in itself a safeguard against slavery to past paradigms, no matter how good they have been.

Even if we choose to develop a wholly new exposition of the tradition, it is wise to be soaked in the past. New models of the tradition do not emerge out of nowhere. They often arise out of the ashes of past endeavors when a creative genius appears and, by the grace of God, strikes out in new directions with a fresh synthesis that unpredictably serves the needs of the hour. There are few such great figures. There may be many who would classify themselves in that league, but this only proves that evangelicals, like other mortals, can have illusions of grandeur. For the most part, it is only possible to identify new exemplars of the tradition in retrospect. Those who set themselves up as new models are prone to develop a messianic complex, which courts self-destruction. It is often wiser to plod the more humble path of patient exposition and fresh articulation. Certainly, it would be a great gain at present were we to possess a fresh exposition of the great historic editions of evangelical theology. It is much healthier to have a set of live options competing for allegiance rather than the modern evangelical orthodoxy, which is presently degenerating into a rigid scholasticism.

Calling Wesleyans to Action

It is in the context of this wide appeal to all evangelicals that I would call upon Wesleyan evangelicals to theological renewal. Given the low estimate accorded Wesley within modern evangelicalism, it is imperative that they set their institutions in order and recover the genius of their tradition. My concern at this stage in the debate is not to spell out the theological details of a new expression of the Wesleyan heritage. This may seem disappointing to some readers. They will be keen to know exactly how I would set out the internal themes of the tradition. They would like to know precisely what I believe about revelation, inspiration, authority, justification, sanctification, atone-

ment, the end times, and the like. I resist the temptation to
write on these topics here not because I am afraid of these issues or because I have nothing to say on these matters. I resist
because at this stage in their history, Wesleyan evangelicals
need to equip themselves more fully as a tradition before they
can hope to meet the demands of the hour. Discerning observers will know in any case that this is not the place for experi-
ments in theological innovation or synthesis.

In other words, the need of the present hour is less to chart
the detailed content of an evangelical theology for the future
and more to call Wesleyan evangelicals to develop comprehensively their own version of the evangelical tradition. If heeded,
this would have a threefold effect. It would confirm the claim
that Wesley really does offer a radically different account of the
heritage from that currently popular. It would inspire the
whole evangelical world to look critically at its roots afresh and
thereby receive greater enrichment. Finally, it would provoke
improvement all around by forcing the opponents of the Wesleyan paradigm to examine it carefully and to produce better
versions of the competing alternatives. What do Wesleyan
evangelicals need to do to have such a salutary effect? They
must first come to terms with the fundamentalist leavening of
their version of the tradition. Thereafter they must take steps to
recover the broader riches of Wesleyan paradigm. Ideally both
of these developments should take place simultaneously.

Countering Fundamentalist Leavening

The impact of fundamentalism and of modern conservative
evangelicalism on contemporary Wesleyan evangelicals
emerges most clearly in the way the latter have developed their
doctrine of inspiration.[1] What has happened over the years is
that conservative Wesleyans, although they have sincerely intended to preserve Wesley's evangelical vision, have abandoned
the tensions and spirit of the classical Wesleyan position and
accepted the modern fundamentalist alternative.[2] Caught be-

tween the extremes of liberalism and fundamentalism, they chose the latter very readily.

The evidence for this is very compelling. Thus the Wesleyan Theological Society (WTS), the scholarly organ of Wesleyan evangelicalism, adopted the following statement on inspiration: "We believe that both Old and New Testaments constitute the divinely-inspired Word of God, inerrant in the originals, and the final authority for life and truth."[3] Not surprisingly, therefore, leading figures in the early days of the WTS took the trouble to parade the standard responses to the usual difficulties with inerrancy.[4] Even Wesley is made to appear as a modern fundamentalist in his doctrine of scripture.[5] Moreover, during the rise and spread of modern evangelical orthodoxy, two major churches in the tradition changed their doctrinal statements on inspiration from the relatively modest claims of the classical period in order to bring them into line with the modern fundamentalist position. Both the Wesleyan Church and the Free Methodist Church took this route, the former in 1955 and the latter in 1974. The actual change as found in the Free Methodist situation is worth documenting, as it indicates that the original statement on scripture does not even include reference to inspiration. Moreover, rather than serving as a doctrinal imposition, it functions to safeguard liberty of doctrinal expression in one's theology. The original states: "The Holy Scriptures contain all things necessary to salvation: so that whatever is not read therein, nor may be proved thereby, is not to be required of any man, that it should be believed as an article of faith, or be thought requisite or necessary to salvation."[6] The present article, by contrast, reads: "We believe the Holy Scriptures are God's record, uniquely inspired by the Holy Spirit. They have been given without error, faithfully recorded by holy men of God as moved by the Holy Spirit, and subsequently transmitted without corruption of any essential doctrine."[7]

A third factor exhibiting the adoption of a fundamentalist view of inspiration surfaced in the in-house reaction to Dewey Beegle's opposition to inerrancy expressed in *The Inspiration of*

Scripture.[8] Beegle argued there that a sound view of inspiration is not dependent on a doctrine of plenary inspiration or on one of inerrancy, neither of which can be sustained by an inductive study of the biblical text. Unfortunately, he gives only the sketchiest indication of how we are to construe inspiration, concentrating his efforts on demolishing the fundamentalist position. Despite that, Beegle is much closer to a Wesleyan understanding of inspiration, revelation, and authority than his fellow Wesleyan critics would allow. What is of interest here is that Beegle touched a raw nerve in conservative Wesleyan circles. A leading bishop in the Free Methodist Church attacked Beegle's views with unabated fervor,[9] while the small intellectual community among free Methodists failed to support him publicly; not surprisingly, he left in due course to join the United Methodist Church. Clearly much of Free Methodism has been deeply influenced by the modern evangelical orthodoxy on inspiration.

Interestingly, conservative Wesleyans did not reach such a point without some resistance, nor is it at all certain that they will continue to accept such a corruption of the classical Wesleyan expression of the evangelical tradition. Paul Bassett argues convincingly that H. Orton Wiley, the leading conservative Wesleyan theologian of the last generation, studiously avoided a fundamentalist doctrine of inspiration in the heyday of the fundamentalist leavening of the tradition.[10] Bassett points out that Wiley quite self-consciously rejected the legalistic defense of the scriptures that ignored the internal witness of the Holy Spirit; such a defense was a hallmark of fundamentalism.[11] Moreover, when in 1928 the Church of the Nazarene came to revise its statement on inspiration, it used some of the fundamentalist rhetoric but carefully shunned the fundamentalist position. Bassett insists that Wiley was the key figure who made this possible.[12] The statement Wiley endorsed, if not wrote, says: "We believe in the plenary inspiration of the Holy Scriptures by which we understand the sixty-six books of the Old and New Testament, given by divine inspiration, inerrantly revealing the will of God concerning us in all things necessary to our salvation;

so whatever is not contained therein is not to be enjoined as an article of faith."[13]

It is worth noting that other conservative Wesleyans writing during the fundamentalist–modernist controversy avoided the fundamentalist conception of inspiration. A. M. Hills, another Nazarene theologian, rejected both verbal and plenary inspiration.

We have stated the two strongest theories of inspiration, the plenary and the verbal, and pointed out the evidence that may fairly be advanced in their defense, in respect to a considerable portion of the Bible. But to say that *all the Scripture* was so inspired, is to put too great a tax upon faith. In view of discrepancies, and disagreements and misquotations, or inaccurate quotation, and the manifestly lower moral and spiritual tone in some passages than in others, these strong theories, if applied to the whole Bible cannot be successfully defended.[14]

Given this, it is not at all surprising that Bassett reports that Hills was considered too liberal with respect to the authority and inspiration of the Bible.[15]

An even better witness against the fundamentalist corruption of the Wesleyan tradition is Solomon Jacob Gamertsfelder.[16] Gamertsfelder, writing in 1921, repudiated the high status that had been attached to the issue of inspiration, stressed the lack of consensus and, while prepared to accept a carefully qualified concept of inerrancy, pointed out that "we must admit the possibility of imperfections in matters not essential to the ultimate aim of revelation."[17] The whole tenor of his theology is generally very far removed from that of the classical fundamentalist literature of the time.[18]

Resistance to the fundamentalist conception of inspiration was by no means confined to the early decades of the twentieth century. On the contrary, there has always been in conservative Wesleyan circles a considerable underground movement against inerrancy. Beegle's book on inspiration was an agressive expression of that spirit. Beegle's concern, as we have noted, was to develop a position commensurate with inductive study of the text. To be sure, following in a noble tradition that stretches from Sanday in the last century down to Barr and Achtemeier in our own, he failed to make the find of innovative move that is needed on this issue. However, his efforts enshrine an indispensable dimension to inspiraton that goes right back to Wesley himself, namely, the concern to relate to the text as it is, rather than how it must be according to our theory. This concern explains in part how it is that conservative Wesleyans in America accepted so readily the tradition of English Bible that developed at Biblical Seminary, New York. This approach to Bible study was once common in American seminaries. It focused on extensive, firsthand, literary study of the Bible in English. Originally, its exponents rather unrealistically hoped that it would provide a third way beyond the extremes of fundamentalism and modernism. Wesleyans took to it like the proverbial duck takes to water.[19] It saved many from fundamentalism and made available a bridge to critical study of the Bible.[20] It also bred suspicion of the deductive, hyper-rationalistic strain in fundamentalism. All this eventually resulted in the ultimate elimination of inerrancy from the doctrinal statement of the Wesleyan Theological Society.[21]

The WTS was not the first Wesleyan institution to reject the fundamentalist conception of inspiration. In 1956 Western Evangelical Seminary adopted the following position on inspiration:

We believe that the sixty-six books of the Old and New Testaments, which the church has universally accepted as the Holy Scriptures, were given by divine inspiration and constitute the revealed Word of God, as the only supreme, sufficient, and authoritative rule of faith and practice, and that the Holy Spirit, who motivated men of God to speak through the written Word, has providentially guarded, in its preservation, the integrity of the message, and continues to illumine the hearts of those who read that they may understand God's redemptive plan.[22]

This view was accepted for several reasons, not the least being because it provided space for Wesleyan members of the faculty who did not subscribe to the inerrancy of the original autographs.[23]

A further indication of resistance to the fundamentalist view of inspiration is the extent to which there has been guarded unease about inerrancy within Free Methodism. It is difficult to avoid the conclusion that this was adopted more because of political pressure from the Wesleyan Church at a time of delicate ecumenical dialogue than because of theological conviction. Certainly, it has not received unanimous approval.[24] Many of the scholars in Free Methodist institutions reject inerrancy without qualification. These form but part of a much wider group of Wesleyans who are seeking to recover and revitalize the best in their own tradition.

Unfortunately, however, this sort of resistance was either ignored or not noticed in the last generation. This was not only natural because even such an influential figure as Wiley shared so much common ground with the fundamentalists that it took keen perception to see the difference between them. Despite Wiley's attempt to develop a nonfundamentalist conception of inspiration, he does not avoid commitment to much of the substance of fundamentalism. He is clearly committed to inerrancy,[25] considers this essential to the authority of scripture,[26] perpetuates the confusion of divine inspiration and divine speaking,[27] and has no interest in and perhaps little sympathy for a critical approach to the Bible. It is small wonder, therefore, that Wiley's writings have been used to transmit a brand of scholastic Wesleyan theology that has left a generation of younger Wesleyans bored with, if not opposed to, systematic theology. To be sure, admirers have argued that Wiley sought to take seriously the whole ecumenical tradition of Christian theology, that he rightly emphasized the primacy of Christ in revelation, and that he never forgot the significance of the internal witness of the Spirit.[28] However, while all this is true, it is difficult to avoid the conclusion that Wiley is more of a scissors-and-paste theologian, putting together various quotations from the past, rather than a creative theologian who exhibits in practice the Wesleyan commitment to scripture, tradition, reason, and experience.[29] Perhaps Wiley's greatest service was to act as a partial lifeline back to Wesley for those conservatives who were deeply intimidated by fundamentalism. If Wesleyan evangelicals are to recover the full riches of their past, however, they must surely heed the warning of Frank Spina of Seattle Pacific University when he writes: "Would it not be cruel irony if we lost our heritage not to the liberals whom we have steadfastly resisted but to fundamentalists whom we have reluctantly courted."[30]

Equipping for the Future

Our brief survey of the treatment of inspiration among Wesleyan evangelicals indicates that many do now recognize the need to break decisively from the strictures of fundamentalism and its modern offspring. Yet this is only a half measure. If a new expression of Wesleyan theology is to emerge from conservative Wesleyan circles, then it is also important that several other steps be taken to enrich and equip those modern evangelicals committed to the Wesleyan paradigm.

First, there will need to be a full recovery, historically speaking, of the total Wesleyan legacy. We need extensive exposure to what Wesley initiated and inspired over the centuries. If Wesleyans encamp on a narrow stream of the tradition, it is likely to remain isolated and unproductive. For example, if everything is made to hinge on commitment to a simplistic doctrine of sanctification or to the modern evangelical orthodoxy on inspiration, then the riches and the spirit of the Wesleyan heritage will have been abandoned. Wesleyans need to soak themselves in the broad river of their own tradition, examining its many streams and tributaries. Yet this should not be done without also submitting oneself to patient and fresh study of the Bible as the fundamental canon of theological and moral reflection. The tradition must always remain subservient to the canon of scripture, a fact conservatives are quick to insist on in theory but slow to exhibit in practice. What Luther once said in his polemic against the Roman Catholic church of his day applies at this point. "We are like men who read the signposts and never travel the road they indicate. Our dear fathers wanted to lead us to the Scriptures by their writings, but we use their works to get away from the Scriptures."[31]

Second, there needs to be bold and unqualified commitment to critical work in biblical studies. At present Wesleyan evangelicals are much too timid in this area.[32] The present danger is that scholars will unconsciously accept the critical orthodoxy of a generation ago, when what is required is a resolute commitment to follow the evidence where it leads. Over time such an ethos could produce its own creative contribution to biblical scholarship. Some, of course, fear that this will devour the riches of the heritage, but this owes more to fundamentalist rhetoric than it does to considered judgment. The fact is we need all the critical wisdom we can muster to hear the full range and depth of the canonical witness. Wedded to sensitive theological reflection, there is no knowing what sound critical study may produce in the providence of God.

Third, there is a need for substantial work in systematic theology. For example, the whole issue of inspiration, revelation, and authority is still a piece of unfinished business. Moreover, the doctrine of prevenient grace needs to be more carefully and precisely articulated, while the issue of sanctification calls for more sensitive, personalistic analysis. Perhaps the whole structure of Wesleyan theology needs to be rethought from the ground up. The work in this area will not be easy, for it is a lean time at present for systematic theology; there is still considerable distrust, so that renewal is taken to involve repudiation; and, to crown it all, the demands laid upon us far exceed those laid upon Wesley.[33] Yet the task must not be shunned, for failure to develop a theological vision will result in Wesleyans unconsciously gravitating to rival theological paradigms.

Last, if all these developments are to take place, then courageous decisions will need to be made in the educational institutions of the Wesleyan tradition. No tradition can survive as a living force without its scholars and, in turn, scholars cannot survive without space, encouragement, and resources. As yet, one looks in vain for a conservative Wesleyan seminary that will venture forth courageously to bring together those diverse elements that Wesley combined to form such an ingenious vision of Christian life and practice. Until this happens the hopes for renewal remain distant if not eschatological.

Let it be noted that such a renewal does not involve the abandoning of those central ingredients of the classical Wesleyan paradigm that have been precious to conservative Wesleyans. The commitments to Jesus Christ as Savior and Lord, the love for the Bible as the Word of God, the pursuit of holiness and spirituality, the passion to spead the gospel to those who need it—all these remain intact as nonnegotiable elements in any future version of the evangelical tradition. On the contrary, the renewal of which I speak will allow these to receive the attention they merit.

Reviewing the Options

In this chapter I sought to chart both the direction and demands of substantial theological renewal. In the end this will involve either the restatement of one paradigm of the tradition or the fresh emergence of a wholly new one. Aware of their own diverse roots, different groups of evangelicals should develop the resources of their chosen historic exemplars in optimum fashion. Failing that, they should take their life in their hands and work out a completely new model of the tradition.

My own preference is to work for a fresh exposition of the Wesleyan paradigm. That new expression, although it must be developed by individual theologians, is ultimately the product of the soil in which it grows. The best soils produce the best theology. Modern Wesleyan evangelicals need, therefore, to accept without apology the integrity and uniqueness of their version of the evangelical heritage. They should purify it of its fundamentalist corruption and expose themselves more fully to the holistic vision developed by Wesley and reworked in various ways by his descendants. They also need to appropriate the full riches of the Bible, boldly using the relevant critical skills to understand its meaning. This in turn should stimulate new efforts in systematic theology. All these developments require courageous and patient support within Wesleyan ecclesiastical and academic institutions. In time such institutions should produce the theologians who will challenge in detail the present model of the evangelical tradition and provoke other evangelicals to articulate even better expressions of the heritage.

In all this, Wesleyans should be the first to remember that theological renewal is but one aspect of the complete renewal that is desperately needed. Wesleyans need to recover not just the genius of the Wesleyan heritage in its theology, they also need to recover its genius for organization, social involvement, ecumenical action, and world mission. For example, the single greatest loss over the years within Wesleyan circles has been the abandoning of the pattern of pastoral care established in the class meetings. Unless this or a modern equivalent is restored within Wesleyan circles, renewal will be mostly cerebral and cosmetic. Without this, young converts will not develop the spiritual stamina needed to survive in the modern world.

Above all, important as theological renewal is, it is not an end in itself. Theology is a servant of the people of God, intended to nurture and express the life of God throughout all creation. For that to develop we need the direct inspiration of the Holy Spirit. To be sure, that inspiration does not operate in a theological vacuum. It is ultimately related to a deep appropriation of the riches of the gospel. Yet, we should be sensitive to the complexity of renewal, including renewal within theology. To be candid, I am not convinced that theological renewal will come until there is a profound spiritual awakening within the church as a whole. This is how it happened with Wesley.

Soaked in the scriptures and the historic faith of the church, willing to open himself with others to God, he found himself at the center of a revival that forced him to think out his theology in fresh and disturbing ways. Even the forms of his presentation were in part determined by the needs of the hour. Who knows what might happen to us all should there be a radical turning to God within our borders.

Anticipating a Great Revival

The present moment is a time for celebration and hope. Just when fundamentalism has emerged again as a noisy option, and just when its neo-evangelical offspring is losing some of its hold on the expression of the evangelical tradition, those evangelicals who know the full riches of their history and the winds of the Spirit should entertain hopes of better things to come. Expressing it most boldly, they should be anticipating a coming great revival.

The signs of that revival are already clear. Among a host of groups within and without the mainline churches, there is an urge for renewal that shows no indications of abating. The charismatic movement, despite its faults, has broken down the old denominational barriers, has fostered dreams of better things to come, has retrieved vital elements of the original gospel message, has vastly extended the ministry of the people of God, and has brought fresh vigor and life to a multitude of defeated Christians. A new generation of young converts has emerged, keen to look critically at the recent past without abandoning the central tenets of the Christian gospel. Thus there is a vast army of new Christians hungry for initiation into a modern version of the Christian faith that will integrate deep piety, social action, and classical theology in a penetrating expression of the Christian gospel. A renewed evangelical tradition that holds in tension both its unity and its diversity can provide exactly this. Seen in all its rich reality, the evangelical past can provide inspiration for the future and space for thought and action in the present. Moreover, the institutional churches are increasingly recognizing that if the church is to be a realistic expression of the Kingdom of God, it needs not just adequate structures, capable leadership, and informed members; it also needs the fresh wind of enthusiastic commitment to God. Renewed and responsible evangelicals can help foster such commitment. Even in the broader culture it is becoming clear that the secularism of the modern world has not delivered the human goods it so confidently promised. Hence there is a greater readiness to look twice at what a revitalized evangelical faith might offer a decaying culture. Evangelicals should seize the hour to think, work, and pray for a major new awakening.

In writing in this manner, I am not offering a triumphalist prediction of what will happen in the near future. There is no knowing how things will turn out; and it is pompous and silly to pretend otherwise. Nor am I at all underestimating the many forces that will oppose evangelicals. Some will consider secularism an irreversible process in the modern culture and construe my suggestions as naive. Some will hold that the evangelical tradition is a minority report that is intellectually bankrupt and thus unworthy of serious attention as a live option for modern Christians. Some will look upon evangelicalism as a cloak for sinister economic and political forces and therefore dangerous in the extreme. Besides such opponents, evangelicals will have to contend with the classical foes of the world, the flesh, and the devil. Thus I am cautious about how things will eventually transpire. All I modestly offer is an expression of hope and a summons to thought and action.

Evangelicals have an honored place in the history of Christianity—especially in those periods of awakening and revival when God has moved mightily to renew the church and spur her on to spread the gospel everywhere, to reform her doctrine and structures, and to seek justice on the face of the earth. We have explored the theological convictions and emphases that informed and sustained the Wesleyan wing of such an awakening. Understanding its rich theological balance, retrieving its

inner spirit, acknowledging its contested character, recognizing
the need to renew its internal dynamics—these are not just the
prelude to revival; they are constitutive of revival itself.

> See how great a flame aspires,
>   Kindled by a spark of grace!
> Jesu's love the nation fires,
>   Sets the kingdoms on a blaze.
> To bring fire on earth He came;
>   Kindled in some hearts it is:
> O that all might catch the flame,
>   All partake the glorious bliss.
>
> When He first the work begun,
>   Small and feeble was His day:
> Now the word doth swiftly run,
>   Now it wins its widening way;
> More and more it spreads and grows
>   Ever mighty to prevail;
> Sin's strongholds it now o'erthrows,
>   Shakes the trembling gates of hell.
>
> Sons of God, your Saviour praise!
>   He the door hath opened wide;
> He hath given the word of grace,
>   Jesu's word is glorified;
> Jesus, mighty to redeem,
>   He alone the work hath wrought;
> Worthy is the work of Him,
>   Him who spake a world from nought.
>
> Saw ye not the cloud arise,
>   Little as a human hand?
> Now it spreads along the skies,
>   Hangs o'er all the thirsty land:
> Lo! the promise of a shower
>   Drops already from above;
> But the Lord will shortly pour
>   All the Spirit of His love![34]

Notes

Chapter 2

1. By far the best treatment of fundamentalism as a historical phenomenon is George M. Marsden, *Fundamentalism and American Culture* (New York: Oxford University Press, 1980). Also worthy of attention is E. R. Sandeen, *The Roots of Fundamentalism* (Chicago: Chicago University Press, 1970).
2. For a helpful summary of the debate on separation, see George W. Dollar, *A History of Fundamentalism in America* (Greenville, SC: Bob Jones University Press, 1973), 280–82.
3. Quoted in Marsden, *Fundamentalism and American Culture*, 38.
4. More recently, fundamentalists have built liberal arts colleges, but these exist in name only, for fundamentalists have no interest in pursuing knowledge for its own sake.
5. The Scopes trial focused on the right of a young Tennessee schoolteacher to teach evolution in a public school. For a judicious account see Marsden, *Fundamentalism and American Culture*, 184–87.
6. Walter Lippman, *A Preface to Morals* (New York: Macmillan, 1929), 31.
7. I am indebted to Farley P. Butler, Jr., for this information. See his "Billy Graham and the End of Evangelical Unity" (Ph.D. thesis, University of Florida, 1976), 92. This thesis is a most helpful account of the transition from fundamentalism to modern evangelicalism, although Farley does not use exactly these categories to describe the change.
8. For a succinct review of the change of name see Harold J. Ockenga, "From Fundamentalism, Through New Evangelicalism, to Evangelicalism," in *Evangelical Roots*, ed. Kenneth Kantzer (New York: Nelson, 1978), 35–46.
9. Especially important were Bernard Ramm, *The Christian View of Science and Scripture* (Grand Rapids, MI: Eerdmans, 1955), Carl F. H. Henry, *The Uneasy Conscience of Modern Fundamentalism* (Grand Rapids, MI: Eerdmans, 1947), and E. J. Carnell, *The Case for Orthodox Theology* (Philadelphia: Westminster, 1959).
10. A full list would have to include Harold Lindsell, Gordon H. Clark, Vernon Grounds, Francis Schaeffer, Everett F. Harrison, Paul K. Jewett, George Ladd, Merrill C. Tenney, Edward J. Young, John Stott, J. I. Packer, Leon Morris, and E. M. Blaicklock. A useful bibliography can be found in Millard Erickson, *The New Evangelical Theology* (London: Marshall, Morgan and Scott, 1968), 237–50. For a fuller list of leaders see Donald Bloesch *The Evangelical Renaissance* (Grand Rapids, MI: Eerdmans, 1973), 30–31. Richard Quebedeaux, *The Young Evangelicals* (San Francisco: Harper & Row, 1974) is also worth consulting, especially 28–37.
11. The better known include Gordon College, Gordon Conwell Seminary, Trinity Evangelical Seminary, and Wheaton College.

12. The key figure in this development is Jerry Falwell, leader of the Moral Majority, a political pressure group in America. The religious content of Falwell's position and its pedigree is usefully documented by insiders in Jerry Falwell, ed., *The Fundamentalist Phenomenon* (Garden City, NY: Doubleday, 1981).
13. Dollar, *A History of Fundamentalism in America*, 383.
14. Quoted in Butler, "Billy Graham and the End of Evangelical Unity," 205. Emphasis as in original.
15. Ibid., 206.
16. For a summary of Henry's position, see Erickson, *The New Evangelical Theology*, 180–88.
17. For a review of present options in eschatology among evangelicals see Robert G. Clouse, ed., *The Meaning of the Millennium: Four Views* (Downers Grove, IL: Inter-Varsity, 1977).
18. Ramm, *The Christian View of Science and Scripture*, 204.
19. Ockenga, "From Fundamentalism," 42.
20. Ockenga rightly points out that division bred further division. A group left Princeton Seminary in 1929 to form Westminister Seminary; a group left Westminister Seminary to found Faith Seminary; a group left Faith Seminary to found Covenant Seminary; yet another group left Covenant Seminary to found Biblical Seminary in Hatfield, Pennsylvania. See Ockenga, "From Fundamentalism."
21. The best study I know is Steve Bruce, "The Student Christian Movement and Inter-Varsity Fellowship: A Sociological Study of the Student Movements," (Ph.D. thesis, University of Stirling, 1980).
22. In J. I. Packer, *"Fundamentalism" and the Word of God* (Grand Rapids, MI: Eerdmans, 1959).

CHAPTER 3

1. Joseph Bayly, "Who Speaks for Evangelicals?" *Eternity* 31 (1980): 55.
2. See Farley P. Butler, Jr., "Billy Graham and the End of Evangelical Unity" (Ph.D. thesis, University of Florida, 1976), 233–35.
3. Ibid., 241.
4. Ibid., 237.
5. Ibid., 203–204.
6. For lucid testimony to this experience see Donald W. Dayton, *Discovering an Evangelical Heritage* (San Francisco: Harper & Row, 1976), 1–5; see also Jim Wallis, *Agenda for Biblical People* (San Francisco: Harper & Row, 1976).
7. See Dayton, *Discovering an Evangelical Heritage*. Dayton's work should be read alongside George M. Marsden, *The Evangelical Mind and the New School Presbyterian Experience* (New Haven, CT: Yale University Press, 1970). Also important is Timothy L. Smith, *Revivalism and Social Reform* (Nashville, TN: Abingdon, 1957).
8. For details on these developments see John S. Olthius et al., *Out of Concern for the Church* (Toronto: Wedge, 1970). The personal cost is well explained in Robert Lee Carvill, "Counting the Cost of 'The New Thing,'" *Vanguard* (March/April 1972): 7–28.

9. Jack Rogers and Donald McKim, *The Authority and Interpretation of the Bible* (San Francisco: Harper & Row, 1979).

10. See, for example, Harold Lindsell, *Battle for the Bible* (Grand Rapids, MI: Zondervan, 1976).

11. See, for example, *Scripture and Truth* ed. D. A. Carson and John D. Woodbridge (Grand Rapids, MI: Zondervan, 1983).

12. This point is well made in Gerald T. Shepard, "Recovering the Natural Sense," *Theology Today* 37 (1981): 332.

13. Carl F. H. Henry, *God, Revelation and Authority* (Waco, TX: Word, 1976–1983).

14. Quoted in Butler, "Billy Graham and the End of Evangelical Unity," 178.

15. Harold Lindsell's latest broadside is *The Bible in the Balance: A Further Look at the Battle for the Bible* (Grand Rapids, MI: Zondervan, 1979).

16. Francis Schaeffer, *The Foundation of Biblical Authority* (Grand Rapids, MI: Zondervan, 1978), 18.

17. Ibid., 19.

18. See Wilbur M. Smith, *Before I Forget* (Chicago: Moody, 1971), 294–95.

19. Ibid., 197. My emphasis.

20. Carl F. H. Henry, "Martyn Lloyd-Jones: From Buckingham to Westminster," *Christianity Today* 24 (1980): 27–34.

21. Ronald J. Sider's most influential book is *Rich Christians in an Age of Hunger* (Downers Grove, IL: Inter-Varsity, 1977).

22. John A. Sproule, "The Social Gospel Invades Evangelicalism," *Spire* 7 (1981): 10.

23. Ibid., 11.

24. See especially Robert Webber, *Common Roots: A Call to Evangelical Maturity* (Grand Rapids, MI: Zondervan, 1978).

25. Robert E. Webber and Donald Bloesch, eds., *The Orthodox Evangelicals* (New York: Nelson, 1978), 20.

26. Ibid., 214.

CHAPTER 4

1. This point is well made by Karl Popper in "Towards a Rational Theory of Tradition," in *Conjectures and Refutations* (London: Routledge and Kegan Paul, 1963), 120–35.

2. See T. F. Torrance, *Reality and Evangelical Theology* (Philadelphia: Westminster, 1982).

CHAPTER 5

1. A helpful modern introduction is Paul Mickey, *Essentials of Wesleyan Theology* (Grand Rapids, MI: Zondervan, 1980.

2. For a very useful introduction see Albert Outler, ed., *John Wesley* (New York: Oxford University Press, 1964).

3. Ibid., vii.

4. See my *The Divine Inspiration of Holy Scripture* (Oxford: Oxford University Press, 1981).

5. I am grateful to Eugene Lemcio for bringing this quotation to my attention.
6. Quoted in A. C. Bouquet, ed., *A Lectionary of Christian Prose* (Derby: Peter Smith, 1965), 73.
7. Quoted in Philip Watson, ed., *The Message of the Wesleys* (London: Epworth, 1964), 185.
8. Ibid., 184.
9. See my *Divine Revelation and the Limits of Historical Criticism* (Oxford: Oxford University Press, 1982).
10. Outler, *John Wesley*, 445.
11. John Wesley, *Forty-four Sermons* (London: Epworth, 1944), 106.
12. Quoted in Mable Richmond Brailsford, *A Tale of Two Brothers* (New York: Oxford University Press, 1954), 208.
13. Quoted in Stanley Ayling, *John Wesley* (Nashville, TN: Abingdon, 1979), 263.
14. Outler, *John Wesley*, 493–99.
15. Ibid., 312.
16. Ibid., 313–14.
17. A splendid descriptive survey of that legacy is given in Thomas A. Langford, *Practical Divinity: Theology in the Wesleyan Tradition* (Nashville, TN: Abingdon, 1983).

CHAPTER 6

1. The most convenient place to locate this thesis is in W. B. Gallie, *Philosophy and the Historical Understanding* (London: Chatto and Windus, 1964), chap. 8.
2. Ibid., 158.
3. Kantzer seems to expand or contract the list at will. The list of sixteen can be found in Kenneth Kantzer, "The Future of the Church and Evangelicalism," in *Evangelicals Face the Future* (Pasadena, CA: William Carey Library, 1978), 133.
4. William W. Wells, *Welcome to the Family: An Introduction to Evangelical Christianity* (Downers Grove, IL: Inter-Varsity, 1979).
5. See Donald W. Dayton, *Discovering an Evangelical Heritage* (San Francisco: Harper & Row, 1976).
6. See my *The Divine Inspiration of Holy Scripture* (Oxford: Oxford University Press, 1981).
7. David Alan Hubbard, *What We Evangelicals Believe* (Pasadena, CA: Fuller Theological Seminary, 1979), 7–11.
8. Donald Bloesch, *Essentials of Evangelical Theology* (San Francisco: Harper & Row, 1978–1979). For a very sympathetic response to Barth, see Gregory G. Bolich, *Karl Barth and Evangelicalism* (Downers Grove, IL: Inter-Varsity, 1980). For complete capitulation to Barth, see Bernard Ramm, *After Fundamentalism* (San Francisco: Harper & Row, 1983).
9. Arminius does not even receive mention in Geoffrey Bromily, *Historical Theology: An Introduction* (Grand Rapids, MI: Eerdmans, 1978).
10. Carl F. H. Henry, *God, Revelation and Authority*, vol. 4 (Waco, TX: Word, 1979), 178.

CHAPTER 7

1. Robert K. Johnston, *Evangelicals at an Impasse* (Atlanta, GA: John Knox, 1979). For an excess of lamentation see John Johnston, *Will Evangelicalism Survive Its Own Popularity?* (Grand Rapids, MI: Zondervan, 1980).
2. Johnson, *Evangelicals at an Impasse,* vii–viii.
3. Ibid., 147.
4. See especially Harold Lindsell, *Battle for the Bible* (Grand Rapids, MI: Zondervan, 1976).
5. E. J. Carnell, *The Case for Orthodox Theology* (Philadelphia: Westminster, 1959), 107–10.
6. Ibid., 110.
7. W. B. Gallie, *Philosophy and the Historical Understanding* (London: Chatto and Windus, 1964), 187–88.
8. I have explored the issue of inspiration at some length in *The Divine Inspiration of Holy Scripture* (Oxford: Oxford University Press, 1981).
9. Gresham Machen, *Christianity and Liberalism* (London: Victory, 1923).
10. Walter Lippman, *A Preface to Morals* (London: Macmillan, 1929), 32.
11. Machen, *Christianity and Liberalism,* 7.
12. George Eliot, "Evangelical Teaching: Dr. Cumming," *The Westminster Review* 64 (1855): 436–37.
13. Sir Edmund Gosse, *Father and Son* (London: Penguin, 1949).
14. Ibid., 246–47.
15. Basil Mitchel, "Indoctrination," in *The Fourth R,* ed. Ian Ramsey (London: S.P.C.K., 1970), 358.
16. Gallie, *Philosophy and the Historical Understanding,* 188.
17. Philippians 1:15.

CHAPTER 8

1. It would be a major study in itself to trace the complex interaction between Wesleyan theology, fundamentalism, and conservative evangelicalism.
2. I discuss the classical Wesleyan tradition on inspiration in "The Concept of Inspiration in the Classical Wesleyan Tradition," in *A Celebration of Ministry,* ed. Kenneth Cain Kinghorn (Wilmore: Francis Asbury, 1982), 33–47.
3. The early issues of the *Wesleyan Theological Journal* printed this as part of the doctrinal statement of the Wesleyan Theological Society. Later it was changed to read: "We believe in the plenary-dynamic and unique inspiration of the Bible as the divine Word of God, the only infallible (i.e. "absolutely trustworthy and unfailing in effectiveness or operation," RHD), sufficient, and authoritative rule of faith and practice." This infelicitous statement was later changed again. See below, n. 21.
4. See Ralph Thompson, "Facing Objections Raised Against Biblical Inerrancy," *Wesleyan Theological Journal* 3 (1968): 21–29; and Wilber T. Dayton, "Theology and Biblical Inerrancy," ibid., 30–37.
5. See William M. Arnett, "John Wesley and the Bible," ibid., 39. Arnett is Professor of Systematic Theology at Asbury Theological Seminary and a loyal defender of inerrancy.

6. *The Doctrines and Discipline of the Free Methodist Church* (Published by B. T. Roberts for the Free Methodist Church, 1860), 18.

7. *Book of Discipline* (Winona Lake, MN: Free Methodist Publishing House, 1979), 13.

8. Dewey Beegle, *The Inspiration of Scripture* (Philadelphia: Westiminster, 1963).

9. See Bishop J. Paul Taylor, "The Inspiration of Scripture, Part I," *The Free Methodist* 96 (23 July 1963): 46; "The Inspiration of Scripture, Part II," ibid., (6 August): 45. Taylor's response was as negative as that of Carl F. H. Henry. See his "Yea Hath God Said . . . ?" *Christianity Today* 7 (1963).

10. See Paul Bassett, "The Fundamentalist Leavening of the Holiness Movement, 1914–1940," *Wesleyan Theological Journal* 13 (1978): 65–91.

11. Ibid., 66–67, 82–84.

12. Ibid., 74.

13. *Manual of the Church of the Nazarene* (Kansas City, MO: Nazarene, 1932), 26.

14. A. M. Hills, *Fundamental Christian Theology*, vol. 1 (Pasadena, CA: C. J. Kinne, 1931), 126.

15. Paul Bassett, "The Fundamentalist Leavening," 80. Bassett thinks that this is surprising, as he believes that Hills is a fundamentalist in his doctrine of scripture. I think he has overlooked Hills's position on the topic of inspiration, while focusing on the absence of any emphasis on the inner witness of the Spirit from his theology.

16. Gamertsfelder worked within the Evangelical Brethren, a German-speaking Methodist group, some of whom later became part of the United Methodist Church.

17. Solomon Jacob Gamertsfelder, *Systematic Theology* (Harrisburg, PA: Evangelical, 1921), 120–21.

18. This is even more true of Hills. Unfortunately Gamertsfelder, who is a much more judicious theologian than either Hills or Wiley, seems to have been forgotten outside a few circles.

19. The most able exponent of English Bible is Robert A. Traina, who teaches at Asbury Theological Seminary.

20. See, for example, Wayne McCown, "Towards a Wesleyan Hermeneutic," *Essays on Hermeneutics*, ed. Wayne McCown and James Earl Massey (Anderson, IN: Warner, 1982).

21. The present statement reads: "We believe in the plenary-dynamic and unique inspiration of the Bible as the Word of God, the only infallible, sufficient and authoritative rule of faith and practice." This is still somewhat heavy handed compared to the more moderate statements of classical Wesleyan theology, but it is an improvement over its predecessors.

22. This is located in the seminary catalogue. The original read: "We believe in the plenary inspiration of the Holy Scriptures, by which we understand the sixty-six books of the Old and New Testaments, that they are the Word of God written, and therefore inerrant in the autographs; that they have been trustworthily preserved by God to be the infallible and authoritative standard of faith and practice, containing all things necessary to our salvation; so that whatsoever is not contained therein nor can be proved thereby is not to be enjoined as an article of faith or made necessary to salvation."

23. For information on this I am indebted to the Presidential report of the Seminary given in January 1978.

24. Bishop Donald N. Bastion is obviously unhappy with the new article. See his *Belonging* (Winona Lake, MN: Light and Life, 1978), 60.
25. H. Orton Wiley, *Christian Theology*, vol. 1 (Kansas City: Beacon Hill, 1940), 167, 172.
26. Ibid., 173.
27. Ibid., 176, 179–80.
28. The former points are stressed by Carl Bangs in *Our Roots of Belief* (Kansas City: Beacon Hill, 1981), 70, 74. Bassett especially focuses on the last point; see "The Fundamentalist Leavening," 68.
29. The generation after Wiley has, as yet, produced little of great significance. One exception worthy of mention is Mildred Bangs Wynkoops's *A Theology of Love* (Kansas City: Beacon Hill, 1972). This is an elusive interpretation of Wesley, but it recaptures something of the freshness of his theology.
30. Frank Spina, "The Scholar as Prophet," unpublished.
31. "To The Christian Nobility," *Luther's Works: The Christian in Society*, ed. James Atkinson, vol. 17 (Philadelphia: Fortress, 1966) 206.
32. A good example of such timidity is McCown's "Towards a Wesleyan Hermeneutic."
33. For further comment see my "The Perils of a Wesleyan Systematic Theologian," *Wesleyan Theological Journal* 17 (1982): 23–29.
34. Charles Wesley, *The Methodist Hymn-Book* (London: Methodist Conference Office, 1933), no. 263.

Index

DATE DUE